NORTH SEA TO THE EAST

for Arjun, Theo and Ajay

so they might know

NORTH SEA TO THE EAST

a personal landscape of teesside and north yorkshire

JOHN POWLS

Red Shoes image by Carol Ballenger

First published in Great Britain in 2020

Copyright © 2020 John Powls

Illustration copyright © 2020 property of the named artists

British Library Cataloguing-in-Publication Data

A CIP record for this title is available from the British Library

ISBN 978 1 906690 73 1

HALSTAR

Halsgrove House, Ryelands Business Park,

Bagley Road, Wellington, Somerset TA21 9PZ

Tel: 01823 653777   Fax: 01823 216796

email: sales@halsgrove.com

An imprint of Halstar Ltd, part of the Halsgrove Group

of Companies. Information on all Halsgrove titles is

available at: www.halsgrove.com

Printed and bound in India

by Parksons Graphics Pvt Ltd

FOREWORD ANTHONY VICKERS

Middlesbrough was not a town built for beauty. It was forged quickly and harshly as a functional framework for the muscle-bound power of the Infant Hercules, and with little thought for the people that would live there, love there and come to call it home.

That harsh environment has spawned a fierce parochial pride in the clang of steel and the fire of industry and in the sweat and skill of the generations that built the world.

For good or ill, this is our town, our identity and the chest swells at the Satanic night time orange glow on the approach from the A19 that scares outsiders.

The Teesside towns huddled in the shadow of the Transporter and in the orbit of Middlesbrough Football Club are no oil painting but they have fostered a unique aesthetic - a distinct approach to art, writing and music born of the harsh realities of a conurbation built to labour and an enticing, sunlit North Yorkshire hinterland that offers an escape.

We are an island of industry amid a lush ocean swell of green, of rolling hills, moors and woods garlanded by heritage coast – our secret to be guarded from the world.

For Teessiders, every view of a cooling tower or sprawl of cracker pipe pumping polyethylene is tempered by a breathtaking gaze across Saltburn Pier at sunset or the rise of Roseberry. They're ours too.

This 'book with the white chestband' – John Powls' collection of his words and artists' images – travels through this cultural contradiction that permeates Teesside sensibilities and powers a rich, colourful and productive vein of art we can call our own.

Anthony Vickers is lately, Senior Football Writer, TeessideLive/Evening Gazette; @untypicalboro

5

CONTENTS

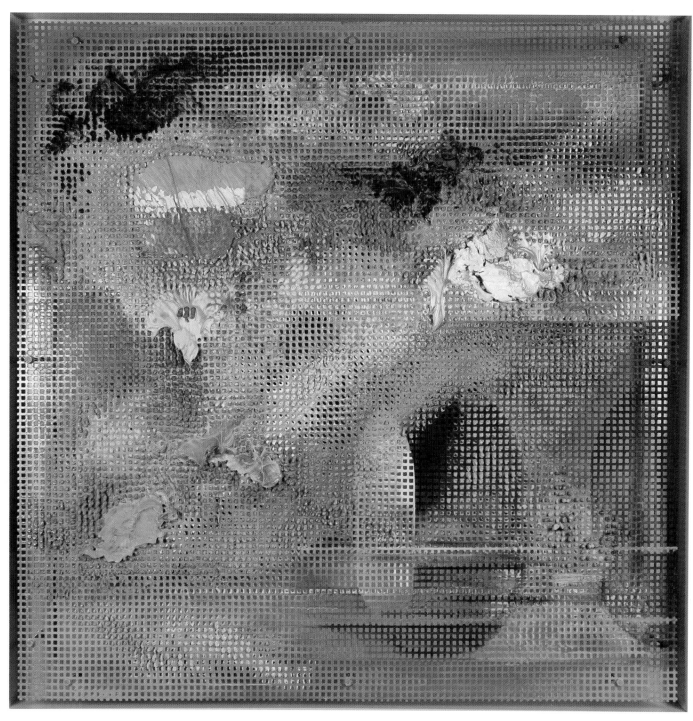

'Relentless: Esk – Relentless 2' by William Tillyer © 2020 William Tillyer

INTRODUCTION JOHN POWLS

'To see clearly is poetry' – J. M. W. Turner

This is a personal landscape of Teesside and North Yorkshire. It is my response to my native landscape which I have known from when I was a boy to revisiting now as a pensioner. The layout of the book follows that timeline.

Poet Norman McCaig asked 'Who owns this landscape?' Well, these are my views but my plan is that the answer is 'as many as share something of an understanding' - if you get my meanings.

Norman answers his own question with another - 'Has it anything to do with love?' My answer to that is assuredly 'Yes, absolutely'. This is a sharing of the heart and a work of time and nature - pastoral, littoral and industrial.

The poems in this collection were written over a period of almost 30 years and cover more than 60 years of my life. It contains the first poem I was paid for, 'Lost', which first appeared in print in 1994, right through to work written as the book was being worked on. But, to paraphrase King Crimson's Robert Fripp, 'For this performance, all the pieces are new'.

There is a strong link between the working processes of poetry and the visual arts which even share a common vocabulary. So, 'North Sea To The East' is also a celebration of the work of many visual artists whose work inspired me with their response to the same landscape. Most are based in or hail from Teesside and North Yorkshire and others are long time collaborators.

I acknowledge the artists individually in the body of the book but it's true to say that this collection of poems would not have been written without their wonderful work and help. My thanks to them is fulsome and heartfelt. The co-operation of galleries, museums, arts organisations and Google has also been key. Images are used with the permission of the copyright holder shown.

Thanks also to my Dad and my sister for all the hunts through diaries and photos and the 'just remind me' conversations as part of my research; to Anthony Vickers for his foreword; to Simon Butler for all his publishing contribution; and, to my family and friends for their encouragement and support.

The excellent Cumbrian poet, Norman Nicholson and his book 'Sea To The West' gave me the original idea for this collection some years ago. I have been wrestling with my subject for as long, with only limited success until recently.

I hope now I have seen clearly.

NORTH SEA TO THE EAST

For William Tillyer and J.M.W. Turner

On the frontiers,
Edge and heart
Tees to Esk,
Epitomised
By mouthtowns;
Cliffedged,
Beachbounded between
And backed
All the way to
Buttertubs by
My green wedge of
North Yorkshire
Discovered,
Worked and won
On common ground;
Noble by purpose
North Sea
To the East

Those rivers,
Stubborn and loyal
In their narratives
Are in us;
Steelgrey
And moonhearted
That sea is
All about us

Waters rendered
Brush and knife
Burnsky and cloudsail
Atmospheres
My mindseye
Tillyer and
Turner landscape
Is

Flux of weather
Full of the music
Of what has
Happened
Fastened deeds
That I hear
As dialogues

Endeavour
The mining,
Making and engineering
Of words;
Product and raw
Material of art
Dark and true
And tender –
Exploring
Faithfully, delightfully
With compassion
Love and wonder

Spirit of place
Development of language
Discovery of voice
Slight of word
Art of the land
To see clearly
Is poetry

The stillness
The shadows
Moving
The everyday creation
The void
Fills
With light and life
Of the land
With
North Sea
To the East

The journey from here
I chose –
It turns out –
Is also the journey
Back here

And always
The uses of poetry

'Relentless: Esk – Ruswarp' by William Tillyer © 2020 William Tillyer

THE FIVE LAMPS

The bold brew of
Walking and words
Came early to me

I loved it when,
Flatcapped,
Grandad said we
We're going
'Over the town'

We stepped out
Down Eric Avenue;
Strong wives washed
And buffed painted
Doorsteps to soft
Lustre, long losing
Their own in
The doing;
Headscarfed, houseproud,
Heartwarm, workworn.
Between the bays
Eddies of winds
Trap the dry leaves
Whirling circling
Spinning round –
I tried to trap
A fixed point
As the world
Turned on tall
Tales – we took a
Turn down a ginnel.

Ordinary times that
Took extraordinary turns
In the telling.

By that landmark
Of gathering,
The Five Lamps,
The Clevo flour mill,
Victoria Bridge
Where I'd stick
My searching fingers
In the sharp
Shrapnel scars
On the wrought
Iron railings,
The old railway
Ticket office,
Before
'The Back Way'
And up Finkle Street
To the High Street,
Stalls and Shambles

Distance seemed
Immaterial – even
To little legs –
Steps sweetened
By stories and
Sucking a
Milady toffee
Discovered in

The dusty recesses
Of Grandad's jacket
Pockets
With a pelt of
Pocket fluff and shreds
Of pipe tobacco

At Great Ayton
Great grandad
Was a coachman
At The Grange and
Ghostly goings on
At Angrove Hall.

Walking to and from
The ore workings
At Roseberry
From Canny Yaton
To put in a shift.
Biking to ICI,
Learning to use
A brush before
Getting on the staff
And getting his watches.

Stories of both wars:
The gas on the front
For Norman

In the one to end them all;
Air warden watches
In the second go –
Crashed German airmen
Respectfully interred
Though their mines –
Exploded and not –
Caused chaos and hurt

The High Green
Harper clan at Stokesley
The bakery at Thornton,
Guisborough gang
And others in
Foreign outposts –
Pickering and Pudsey.

Then tall tales
Of derring do
And adventure around
The globe and near
His back yard.

Each embroidered
With a little more
Colour and pattern
On every walk
Not sampler neat
But at tapestry scale.
Like being read
A book at bedtime

12

I never wanted him
To miss even a bit
And never tired
Of hearing them again.

All too soon we were
Back to Park Avenue
Via Teesdale and Bill Smith's

Fish, fishcake and chips
With buttered
Bread buns,
All washed
Down with Lowcock's
Lemonade
Cool from the concrete
Pantry floor in the
Scullery –
What Gran
Would call
'A good feed'
And she knew
How to feed folk.

I was filled up

The Five Lamps, Thornaby, 1957 © 2020 Francis Frith Collection

Thornaby on Tees, composite postcard, 1960 © 2020 Francis Frith Collection

Images of Stockton Market c. 1957 by Tony Whelan.

© 2020 Tony's son, Nick Whelan and reproduced with his kind permission and technical support.

LOST – THE SHAMBLES, STOCKTON MARKET 1956

For Tony and Nick Whelan

Stockton High Street
That great, broad
Breath of fresh air;
Age three
The Saturday market
Was a deckchair striped
Analogue of paradise.
Flowers, fruit and fish,
Loose sweets and
Broken biscuits,
Crockery clatterclinking,
Cheap magic, anticipated.
Intoxicating,
Structured stalls,
Shouts, smells, symbols –
Means of proclaiming
The rituals
Of bargains and banter.
Entrancing.
Until I lost
My father's hand.
Artificial paradise
Made real hell.
My panicked
Knight moves,
Dislocated,
Emptied by loss;

Dwarfed by the loud
Mechanics of chaos
Exploiting the potential
Of their uncaring height.
A moving maze
With no exit.
Stopped short,
Shambles snared,
Where skinned rabbits
Stare blankly as
They ooze onto
Sticky sawdust......
DADDY!

THE PERSISTENCE OF WALKING
For Peter M. Hicks, Peter and Lesley Hough

There is a compact
Between walking
And writing –
A walk is only
Ever a step away
From a story
And every path tells
In its way.

Keeping my part
Of that bargain,
Appreciating
The privilege,
I have walked
Myself to poems;
Stride by stride
Getting the measure
Of my narrative –
A yardstick

Representing landscape

Weather and
Way, sublime
Airs over water,
Light through trees
Skyisland clouds –
Moving, all –

Enfolding and opening
Emotion finds and fills me
Making my words
Worth.

By the terms
Of agreement,
Fulfilled, at last,
In contemplation,
I make marks
Of my recollection;
A dragonfly companion.

From 'Entrance to a Lane' by Peter M. Hicks © 2020 Peter M. Hicks by kind permission of Peter and Lesley Hough.

DOWN THE BECK

For 'BB', Mackenzie Thorpe and 'My Little Pal'

Some years our Spring
Seemed late with hawthorn
Blossom blown with the
Last fallen cold petals, both
Skyflowers of slow Winter
White snowscent dressing
First grassgrowth and crocus

Hedge budded but brittle;
Furrowed field beyond, bitten
And bare like black branched
Bushes; but, under bark and in
Stem and root boiled pent
Up power of countless leaves;
This year's growth, relentless

And, us, Lowcock's fit to fizz
Over - then those heady days
At Spring's first warmth
We were turned out by Mams,
Told 'don't stray too far away', but
You could go 'Down the beck'
And stay there for the day

Intrepid, we were as we ran
Everywhere, kneebark free
Laboured without complaint
At dam building, stick
Gathering and stone crop, all
Mutable elements of making
Our mark on this growing world

We were explorers of a
Cold jungle and flew the beck
On frayed rope or cap gun cowboys –
White hats, black hats and 'the girl',
Imagined like our proud palominos.
All in our placings, never spoken
But our part deeply understood

Once grown, that landscape set
Child's simple play delights
Of grass and trees and tarzys;
Talking water, echoing bridges
Bugs, birds and big ideas
Can all be lost to dull cares
Dusty days and duty calls

Unless.......

Image © 2020 Reach Plc; with kind permission from Teesside Live

When we moved there in 1955, Brookfield was aptly named – the few homes and roads early in the new Duncanson brothers development either paralleled or crossed a brook, or beck, running through the fields of Ulla Farm just beyond the outer terminus of the A bus.

What was then a close of twelve houses were mostly occupied by young families and, so, we acquired a ready made gang and the safe outdoors freedom of the sort of landscape of childhood that only seemed to come from the pages of Enid Blyton. Not for the first time, I count myself lucky.

'My Little Pal' by Mackenzie Thorpe © 2020 Mackenzie Thorpe Ltd

THE MASHAM

For my late, much missed Mam – thanks for everything

Brown and green,
The salt glazed tiles.
Wreathed red triangle.
Glass, frosted and stained,
Etched with the names
Of minor pagan deities,
Sacred to manhood.
The dangerous scent
Through the open door
Unlocks from memory
A forbidden land
From childhood.

Hand in white-gloved
Conspiracy
With my mother
We hurried by
At respectable speed.
The taproom of
The Masham.
That rich mash, pooled;
Rum and best bitter,
Plug twist and navy cut,
Used oil, coke,
Worksweated overalls
And damp, varnished
Mahogany
With the spice
Of big stories,

Scored with words
I knew better
Not to know –
Nana Madge wouldn't
Have stood for it from
Behind her bar
At The Bridge
Over the border

And Grandad Tom
Was a gentleman –
Mam said.

Now I see those
Sounds and smells
Deconstructed,
Experienced, rationalised.
Then....
I secretly thrilled
To them as
The spoor
And swagger
Of warriors.

'The Masham Hotel' by Lynne@SmoggieArt © 2020 SmoggieArt

SCARBOROUGH

Back then
We didn't have
Much
But then we
Weren't aware
Because no-one
We knew had
Much
Either.
In what mattered,
We were
Haves
Not
Have nots
Though
Much
Was in short
Supply generally
But you could get
By
And
By
And
By
A level of
Much
Would come
And with it
Change.

Not all of that
Would matter
Much
But the same
Things were
Worth more

By gone
Would
Be bygones

Back then,
Between
By
And
Much
But
Much
Closer to
By
Was always still
A holiday
And back then
A holiday
Was always
Simply splendid
Scarborough –
It was as
Far as we knew.

And Scarborough
Was always
Foreign
Familiar
Family
50's
Neon and Greys**
And we were
Abroad –
Technicolor,
Laughter and
Lemontop,
Salty lips and
Sticky fingers
Abroad –
And a week
Was excited
Endless
But too short
It was as
Far as we knew
And further

I still have
That sand
In my shoes

**some shades of 'back then' Scarborough grey

* Peasholm Park Naval Battle ship grey
* holiday let net curtain grey
* North Sea greys with Coronia dip, breast, butt and roll
* clothes, washed and better washed grey
* streaks of cloud that would be red sky at night greys
* any gadge on the beach rolled up trouser grey
* unspecified 'meat' grey
* wet Castle grey
* North Bay open air pool seawater froth by dinner time grey;

set off by:
* indefinable darker sludge on the floor of the changies and in the slipper bath grey
* holiday snaps you could still picture the colours in grey
* morning mist down on Oliver's Mount ready to lift grey
* Grandads' flat cap grey
* fluff on long hoarded, half unwrapped toffees grey
* knitted cozzie grey
* rare treat Corner Cafe dank day fag fug grey

'Grisaille – Giving Ground Gently to Greater' by Lindsay Mullen © 2020 Lindsay Mullen

BEOWULF

One key event in sparking my interest in and influencing my later career in poetry was experiencing the oldest known poem in Old English, 'Beowulf', being brought to life by my teacher, Miss Walker, at Whinney Banks Junior School when I was aged 10.

She read the poem to us with the gusto it demands – largely in translation but from time to time in Old English. She encouraged us to read aloud to the class, mostly from the translation.

But some of us also read short passages learned phonetically from a reading of the first written text – a means not dissimilar to the oral tradition of transmission and performance of the poem in its likely origins.

It opened a world to me that was thrilling, engaging and inspiring with a language and landscape I instinctively understood, with coming from Teesside conferring certain inherited cultural advantages in that.

I have carried many of the traits of that Old English grammar and approach into my poetic practice and employ them to this day. Every poem that I commit to paper has been performed out loud several times. Each time I perform work in public it changes subtly.

I read an interpretation of 'Beowulf' at least once a year and joyfully struggle through annotated passages of the original, declaiming them out loud!

My favourite modern interpretation is that by Nobel Laureate for Literature and poet, Seamus Heaney. It is a poetic work of art in its own right but, to me, gets closest to the spirit of the original both as a written piece but also when performed.

In recent years, Dr. Janina Ramirez has produced an accessible and authoritative book in the Ladybird Expert Series which gets to the essence of the Old English poem, it's language, world and context with the sort of passion and precision that Miss Walker epitomised all those years ago and which has stimulated me to pursue my interest even further.

I thank all three of these mentors for my work and, hence, the poem is dedicated to them.

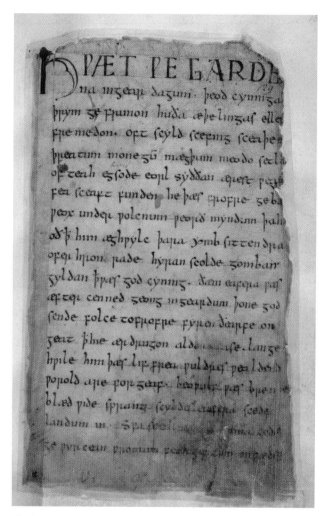

Original Beowulf text © 2020 British Library

WHINNEY BANKS JUNIOR SCHOOL – READING BEOWULF OUT LOUD

For Miss Walker, Seamus Heaney and Janina Ramirez

'Kwaet',
Declaimed Miss Walker,
Our scop*
For the morning
And the lesson
Took the air.
'Poetry is made
In the mouth
And shaped
In the ear –
Out loud.
The uses of poetry
Are many for
Writer, reader
And listener'

Like Codex scribes
We struggled
To follow, as
Vowel-shifters,
The tongues
Of our forefathers;
Transported
From the classroom
To Hall Heorot
In the longboat
Fashioned
From bent tube
And plywood
Desks
Deepscored

With scatology
Of generations
The rhythm of
The half-line
Pulling on oars

Our epic:
North Sea
To the East,
Deep in Danelaw
Side of sail-road,
Seal-road, keel-road
Riverrun
Surrounded
By scarred
And lovely
Landscapes
Namebranded
Of old English
And Scandinavian.
No child of Teesside
Needed much
Imagination
To recognise
The enclave along
Our river
Where 'water burned'
'Sky wept' and
'Hot gore' or ore
'Oozed from earth'
As a place where

Shadow-walkers were
Ready to threaten
Hall and home
And where our heroes
Ventured daily
To battle and
Trade their safety
In search of honour
And hoardgold.
Celebrated long
And loud
They did, but
Returned to tip
The gelt to their
Pursekeeper –
Bairnbearer
Hearthqueen and
Heart's envoy.
We knew many
Of our number
Owing
Would follow their
Lead in our turn
This is the way
The bonds were
Forged
And iron
Shieldwall stood
Our worldplace,
Weighing how much
Words can hold.

For me,
A new weapon
And way ahead
Was being forged
Out of the
Familiar

Unlocking that
Wordhoard
By heart and rote
I will learn that
My words are
Binding one
To the other
Building beauty
Poetry enchanted
Gold immutable

Soundsibling, sibilant
Letterlinked, Kenningkeen
Heartleapt, Whisperwind

To mouthmake
And earshape
Stories shared
Love of our Landscaef
A safe place
For imaginations
To grow.

*Scop: Anglo Saxon minstrel

'Beowulf Sets Sail' by Jacob Sharpe © 2020 Jacob Sharpe/thehangingbadger

THE SEADOOR AND THE SLEEPING HILLS

Close and handsome curve of river, cross coastal plain. Seadoor. Steers the gaze to the scarprise of sleeping hills

'The Tees with the Cleveland Hills' by J.M.W. Turner Turner Bequest, Tate Britain; digital photo © 2020 Tate

ACKLAM HALL GRAMMAR SCHOOL – THE LIBRARY

Place of oaks.
Pull back from
Long shot of
Avenue of trees
Lime, beech, pinelined
Shaping perspective
By design
Move horizon closer
Encircling limit,
Beckoning edge.

Focus close
On the motes
That float like ideas
In the still library air
Stirring slow
By low slant
Of afternoon sun
Reflecting on
Polished surfaces,
Stacked shelves serried;
Indexed backdrop
Of once distant giants
Brought close
To intimidate with
Size and age but
Offering shoulders
Set square for
A new invented
Life to stand on

I was a reader;
Time was away –
In secular silence
My first attempts
To craft
An intimate epic
Concerning
Understanding
And reluctance,
The lies that are
And will be
The truth
Masked and
Unmasked;
Art concealed in
Artifice.
What it hinges on:
No hiding;
The young man's
Enthusiasms
And certainties

The search for
The general
In the particular
With fascination
For the intricacies;
A miniature machine
For mixed meanings
With many
Moving parts

The power and
Precision of poems
To focus, tight, on
The small things
And then open
Out – cut to wide shot –
Vividly elemental
And sublime;
The words
Magnificently
Unadorned
In the doing.
Senses and essence
Out of the ordinary.

Reading between
The lines
As I'm making
It up
But what falls
Into the gaps
And is lost?

Nothing

Hidden shallows
Would muddy
The waters
For the illusion
Of depth;

Mountains of self,
Monumental,
Dull edifices
Of causes
Carved out
Undistinguished;
Wood for the trees;
Best left.

Question remains
Hanging in
The bookbound air –
'Will I?'

And the writing
Of some blazered
Philosopher
Cut deep
Into panelled
Wall says
'You're here –
Now what?'

I know my answers
By heart;
I am a writer, yet
In search of
My voice
Learn to do;
Do to learn;
Do better.

Experience is moving,
Dimensioned by
History and geography
There to be read;
Peopled places, land
And sea make
Marks on memory
Somewhere between
Neglect and obsession –
Nothing intended –
On which I
Will graft my
Present meaning
Inspired

'Aut nunquam tentes aut
perfice'

Establishing shot
Lengthens through
Library window
Of opportunity
Down the drive,
Avenue of trees
And on......

'Window of Opportunity' by Lynne@SmoggieArt © 2020 SmoggieArt

AVENUE OF TREES IN THE SNOW

For Eamonn McGovern

Confronted
By beauty
The long shadow
Stark skeleton
Of a single tree
Etched in frost
On the sharp grass
In wallshade before
The great gates arc.
Recent rote recited
Hopkins' shivelights
Lance into thoughts

Suddenly
Clean, blue air
And the folds
Of fresh snow
Stacked sheer
Like bolts
Of white silk
Billowed
Against black
Boles of lime
Spilled
As if for show
To the middle
Of starker lines

Beech and pine
Blueshadowed

Pristine
It almost seemed
A shame to spoil
By schoolboy
Steps
As the sparkle
Of hoar frost
Danced down
From host branch
Shivering above

But then
There'll be a
Breakneck slide
In the quad and
Always a game
Of footy.
So, press on;
Make tracks

And the silver
Powder starts
Up

'Avenue of Trees in the Snow' by Eamonn McGovern © 2020 Eamonn McGovern

TEENAGE HEARTBREAK

For Samuel Beckett

Waiting

A country road
A tree
Evening

Who bonds
Shoulder to shoulder
Best?

Never betrayed
The heart that
Loves

So, I bond
With the road
Alone

Space for
The sense of
Quiet

My landscape
By myself
Learned

When whispers
Of better come
Gently

Resolved

The 'Teenage Heartbreak' poems and images on these and the following two pages are inspired by the lone tree, close to Roseberry Topping –
For Richard Spare

'Teenage Heartbreak – Beckett' by Richard Spare © *2020 Richard Spare*

TEENAGE HEARTBREAK TOO

So nearly a renga for Sylvia Plath

the leaf fall of words
stream of reflection the stained
glass hues of moods; win

dow on a world glows
true beauty from light within
expression inspired

bare black hawthorn stretched
along the wind sinuous
dancer's memories

a small polished stone
sinks straight through the darkening
waters of your heart

'Teenage Heartbreak – Plath' by Richard Spare © *2020 Richard Spare*

TEENAGE HEARTBREAK 3

For Leonard Cohen; Punch a tree

Smokesky sunset
Bramble, baked earth
Drying drawn blood; barked

Cold fired by the
Crescent moon
Cuts a slit in the sky

The wounds of follies
Kept open. Make believe
Is make   believe

'Teenage Heartbreak – Cohen' by Richard Spare © *2020 Richard Spare*

NIGHTWALK – LEALHOLM

Up the hill, then
Off Eller Gates
The world
Has turned
Lead-silver
And slate
Under blue-black
Sky
Where darkness
Is more itself
And a thousand
Acres of mist
Rises to make
New islands
Of humpback hills
Heathershawled
In black
Ridge trees
Snag the moon,
Branches dreamlit.
Somewhere
A stream.
Woodsmoke
Earth, bracken, grass
The rich and
Certain
Of the day
Unveiled

To strangeness
Welcomed.
Not home
But a warmlit folly
Much desired –
No country for
Young men.

I can feel
The air
Like being wrapped
In clean cold dark raw
Silk
And the long,
Slow pulse
Of the land
Everything is
Noticeable

But not by
Eyes turned
Down and
Slowing steps
Allowed by
Audible margin
Of the path
Where grass
Lengthens

And small stones
Gather
Footfall stills;
Hunched rocks
With moss pelts
Crouch, hurt
Over secrets.
Badger bark
Struck against
The black
Moontempted moths
Prey silence
Dark exchanges
Foxamber and owl
Hushwinged
Catpaused silent
Choreography
Of pipistrelles
Hunting
Tuned to higher
Things

Nearing windows
Butter yellow
Beckoning
With lamplight
Home and hearth
For this new night

Breathheld
Reduced
Simplified
Distilled
Essential

Questions of
Place and character
Night walk's
Purpose achieved

That outrageous
Voice

'Relentless Esk – Lealholm' by William Tillyer © *2020 William Tillyer*

MOONLIGHT AND SNOW – PERSPECTIVES

For Mackenzie Thorpe

The steel breeze
Stilled
The sky was blue-
Purple hazed like
The blush on
An over-ripe plum
In Grandad's garden –
At least that's
What me Dad said
As we huddled closer;
I think on this
Start of images
River's reflections –
Reverent the closing
Clouds
Threw cloak around
The growing
Dark.
We grow, quiet;
Stilled

I see the possibilities –

Sometimes sound
Cuts the silence
Sometimes silence
Cuts the sound
Sometimes silence
Is the sound;
Directed

Both demand
Attention

Mooncushioned, resting
Girded around; girdered;
Rhymed, pallidly
By inadequate, cold lamps

And the hushed panes
That once spoke lightly of
Silver and gold
But not always warmth
Within
At least, not for me
Melancholy

Greyfaced
Clenched like
Cold fists
Against a thin
Wind, hinting

All incomplete
Needing a
Resolving idea
To give emotion
Form and control
I imagine

Was there a better
Way
To express love
Than to just
Come out with it

Works of translation;
Bridges

I see the possibilities –

Together and apart,
The usual heart left
Where, red, it is easily
Found and read
And sometimes,
Starcrossed,
Slowfall

And so, we're
Left with
Moonlight and snow

Unusually for me the poem inspired by this image by Mackenzie is written in two voices – the boy in the bobble hat and the bloke on the staithe, midground.

'Snow on the Tees' by Mackenzie Thorpe © 2020 Mackenzie Thorpe Ltd

THE CRICKET GROUND – GREAT AYTON

The Proust effect:

Pint, pen and phone
In the pavilion –
Roving report
Down the line
On league cricket
For local radio

Between innings I
Stroll round the
Boundary rope
Trying my balance
When I think
No-one's looking.
Then reverie rises
With the soft
Sunstirred smell
Of grass mowings
Heaped where the
Meadow reclaims
The ground

Packed in
Grandad Palmer's
Old Hillman
Park up in
High Green
Pause to pick up
Petch pork pies
Perfects the picnic.

Across the bridge
Through the field
By the Leven
Over the stile
Under cloudland
Blue
As the sound of
The game grows
Closer.

Find your spot
Outside the ropes
Spread the blanket
Broach the thermos
Break into the grub
A later lap or two
Of the boundary
Brings energy
Back in bounds
For French Cricket
Bare legged wicket
At tea in the proper
Game barely seen
Then retrace steps
Back to the car
But not before
The scene closer
Cold and creamy
Suggitt's cornets.
The cool taste of
Childhood

Full circle to
Those same
Grass clippings –
Scene lap fades;
Slips back to
Sanctuary seeking
Grandad Tom's
Greenhouse humid
With its beadhung
Breath of heatmoist
Peat and pipe smoke
Vinecurled over
Tomato tendrils
Reaching to ripen;
Absorbing, quiet
As a book

Growing

Reawakened
By whites crossing
The ropes to square –
Back to the
Pavilion, plotting
The pithy, the pun
The pleasantry
Leavening precision

Temps perdu

'Dad's Hillman'
© 2020 John P. Powls

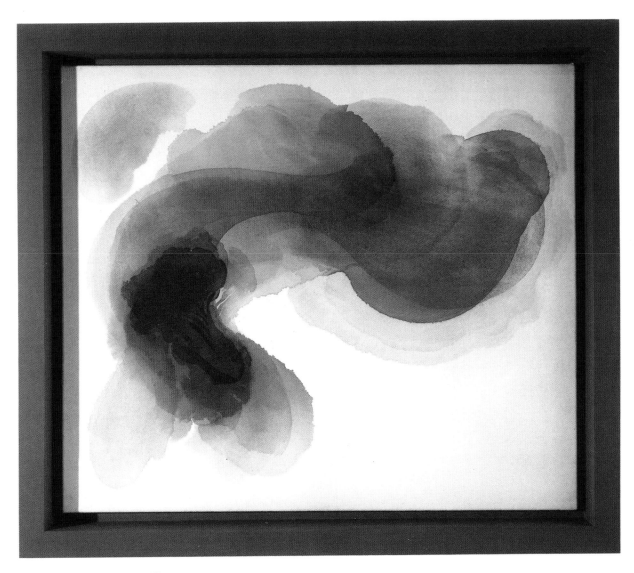

'Ayton' by William Tillyer © *2020 William Tillyer*

TRIPTYCH FOR AN INDUSTRIAL ALTAR PIECE – REDCAR BLAST

For my Dad and David Watson

Like many Teessiders, after his National Service and a short spell at ICI, my Dad worked for Dorman Long then British Steel – and its many successors – for 47 years. It's what you did.

He started 'on the tools' as an electrician and finished as operations engineer. He was based at various works – Acklam, Clay Lane, Lackenby and Redcar Blast as the business moved inexorably downriver towards the mouth of the Tees.

It would be fair to say that, like many, he 'enjoyed' a love/hate relationship with the industry where he earned the wage that, eventually, gave his family the comfortable living standard we enjoyed. It's what he did.

My Mam used to say, though, that he polished the machinery with his hankie so she had a view on which side of the love/hate balance she felt he was, mostly!

'A man becomes what he does', they say – and, 'what he does becomes a man'. True of the best of men.

The now elegiac, official photographic image of Redcar Blast at the time of his retirement still has a pride of place on his dining room unit – history made visible.

At every site he worked, Dad took me to visit. I guess the reason for that was equal parts about education, appreciation and warning as my schooling and university career progressed.

The poems that complete this triptych, this altar piece to a dying but still potent deity, deal with the last of those visits – to the Redcar Blast Furnace complex.

Like all the sites I visited with Dad, Redcar Blast is now cold – coincidence not causality, I like to think!

Unlike the others, at time of writing, it still stands – a major industrial historical artefact no less magnificent or important than any medieval castle of the North East dominating the coast it defended and supported. History made visible.

Though there are laudable plans to deliver smaller scale steelmaking, carbon capture and other industry on the site now back in public ownership the Redcar blast plant isn't coming back with its original function.

So, I argue, why not do those good new things but also treat the furnace as the English industrial heritage it undoubtedly is and preserve it, retaining the main furnace framework made safe and turning its reclaimed grounds and some river mouth frontage to public parkland and nature reserve and poisoned soil to growing.

Westphalia, Germany has done this to great present/future effect – deriving economic and environmental benefit and jobs in the process – with the Duisburg Nord plant. It's what several other countries have also done. It's what we could do. As I write, though, the work of clearing the site has started.

TRIPTYCH FOR AN INDUSTRIAL ALTAR PIECE – LEFT PANEL
REDCAR BLAST – FURNACE

For Dad – with thanks for, well, everything

Tourist of an
Industrial landscape.

Walls, towers, battlements
Steel stalwart of the strand
Castling the iron throne
Of a dynasty already
Dying but did not
Know it then –
Constant, the anxiety
Of hope –
The bastard line
Of Ironmasters
And Infant Hercules,
Bridgenamed
The world over.
Keep deep,
Blast and counterblast
Against many a monstrous
Regiment?
At the burning heart
Charging and casting
Daylong, nightlong.

From the furnace top
The highest ramparts
Even
The North Sea
By the Gare

Is evened out
And almost neat
A drawn out broad
Lacy fan of froth
Were it not
Steel grey and
Flecked molten
By flare stack –
Inland,
The cooling towers,
Mid-distant, fearful
Factories for forming
Clouds, billowing.
Suddenly, silent
Against smokesky
Over the Nab
The swirling, inky
Thumbsmudge
Of starling
Murmuration
Mirrors steam
And smokeshroud
Acrid surrounds
The raw and material
Then and now.

Conveyors churn
Continuous charge
Feed the furnace

While, at ground,
More belts have
Their measure –
And mine –
As I clutch the rail
Just too tightly –
It stood for all –
And trust the
Latticed walkway
While I whistle
In the growing dark
Tune torn away
Over Teesmouth
By whipping wind.

Far below
Sleek black school of
Whale-torpedos
Move sinister slow
Line astern
On track
Nurturing the fire
In their belly.
And everything
Competes with
Everything else
To make a noise
As brutal as its size
And blackened bulk.

Equal parts education,
Appreciation and warning –
Lessons in life.

To learn; to
Break away;
To transcend;
End

'Smoke, Sky, Industry' by David Watson © *2020 David Watson*

TRIPTYCH FOR AN INDUSTRIAL ALTAR PIECE – CENTRE PANEL
CAST HOUSE FLOOR – THE BELLY OF THE BEAST

Down here
In the belly
Of the beast
Where the work
Gets done
Molten metal
Golden
Runs like a
Scorching Styx
Steel river that
Carries faces
Surfacing from
The swift smelt

In these bowels
Heavy duffel-coated
Attendants dance
Tapping
In flickering ritual
Routine
On the casting floor
Thrown
In sudden stark relief
Repel the slag
Skimmed sparks,
The reports of water
On rogue iron

And everywhere
The gas chance.
Here they make
What made the World
And
The legendary thirst
That had been slaked
At the Mucky Pots
Once the shift's
Last plug is
Swung in and
The seamless
Changeover
And before the
Toil and trouble
Scum skinned
Ladled slag's
Set solid on its
Heap

Sparks that set
Silver in air
Shower like stardust.
Like that sharp
And sparkling
Cast house dust
That covers all
Do I settle on this town
Or do I blow?

Grit in the eye
Makes you cry.
Steeling myself

Stardust, golden
Billion year old
Carbon
Iron from a starheart
Collapsed and exploded
Heavy elements
At last
As the light dies.

Beyond events
Horizon
What escapes
From this black hole
Is the chance
To renew

*Opposite: 'Belly of the Beast' by
David Watson* © 2020 David Watson

TRIPTYCH FOR AN INDUSTRIAL ALTAR PIECE – RIGHT PANEL
REDCAR BLAST COLD

Tourist of an
Industrial landscape
Revisited.

Now cold,
A still life
At monumental scale
That befits
Sublime, becoming
Landscape –
Disenchantment
To re-enchantment
It stands
Of history and imagination
Made visible.

Reclaiming
Black birch branch
Slender silver trunk,
Hazel twigs turn and
Purple alder thin; quick
Hawthorn thick set gnarl
Stretched along the wind -
Stand for robinsong;
Territorial. Already
Furrowed oaks, callow
But patient as
Old friends, yet
Just shoulder high

In their nakedness,
Beauty
As sunlight seeps in
Stark and exposed
Share special
Intimacy
With the cold ovens
And frigid furnace
Tall, gaunt and bare
Interpreting the airs
Off the Gare
That brustle tenacious
Grip of grasses
The colour of
Cablerust
And rattle the
Bony branch claw
That scratches at
Thin air

The lone gull
Settled on staithe
Skeleton stump;
Suddenly, silent
Against smokesky
Over South Gare
The swirling, inky
Thumbsmudge
Of startled sandpiper
Murmuration meaning

Stirring symbols;
The air swept clean
Above Paddy's Hole
And Coatham dunes.

Suffering of silent stone,
Slag and steel
In thin snow asks
Where does
This land stand
As its world turns
Searching for
Consolation in
Poetry read between
Moss softened lines
Of abandoned tracks.

Steeling itself,
The watergather
In the broken roadway
Pothole pond
Reflects on cusp
Of crystalline –
Thaw and solid,
Narrow margins
Patterns beauty

Like that sharp
And sparkling
Hoar frost dusting

That covers all
Settles to wait
The turn when
Days get longer

No wonder
Gutsy goldfinch
Tease teasel
Fissle
As they flicker
In flight and fight.
Charm

The raw light
The delicacy,
Accuracy and power
Of a hard green love
Urgent and stronger
Than steel
Making new;
Making good.
Grows
Sure as Spring

Man made,
It's natural
To build on –
Palimpsest of place –
Allow the future
To present itself.

'The Chapel of Rest' by David Watson © 2020 David Watson

TRIPTYCH COUNTERPOINT – ALLOW THE FUTURE TO PRESENT ITSELF
REDCAR BLAST COLD – RENAISSANCE – THE BIRDS RETURN

For Richard Spare

'Winter Robin' by Richard Spare

Stand for robinsong;
Territorial

'Lone Gull' by Richard Spare

The lone gull
Settled on staithe
Skeleton stump;

'andpiper Murmuration' by Richard Spare

'Goldfinch' by Richard Spare

humbsmudge
f startled sandpiper
lurmuration meaning

No wonder
Gutsy goldfinch
Tease teasel
Fissle
As they flicker
In flight and fight

THE GUIDING STAR – AT PADDY'S HOLE, SOUTH GARE, REDCAR

For Matt Whitfield and John Masefield

From what use-tattered primary school anthology did I first catch
Masefield Sea Fever? Committing it to memory by heart so surely
That first sight of this Redcar coble, inexact as its timeless name is
In that context, still provokes me to recite all three rolling verses

Without hesitation, even as the thin wind out of the North East cuts
Over the Gare like his whetted knife. And tide's clear call while grey
Mist shifts from face of South shore of sea door, welcome and fare
Well, where sea and Tees, brine and brackbrown, form flowing trinity

With opening sky. Down again, are we heading, true, for this haven
Of a haven made or rushing to the reckoning? This marginal land-
Scape shaped of words, work and waters' ways debatable; creeled
A catch for me of purpose, passion and romance. Our way home, found.

And all I ask....

'Guiding Star, Paddy's Hole, Redcar' by Matt Whitfield © *2020 Matt Whitfield*

Backstage PASS

REDCAR JAZZ CLUB

Dennis **Weller** Chris Scott **Wilson** & Graham **Lowe**

ALAN FEARNLEY

RECORDS

FOLK BLUES and JAZZ

THORPE ROAD, MIDDLESBROUGH
Telephone 45520

☆ THE REDCAR JAZZ CLUB ☆
COATHAM HOTEL   7 p.m.   THE   THIS SUNDAY

PINK FLOYD

PLUS

THE SILVERSTONE SET

Members 7/-   Guests 8/6

REDCAR JAZZ CLUB ☆
HOTEL   7 P.M..   THIS SUNDAY

The BONZO DOG DOO DAH BAND

Plus THE MONTANAS

MEMBERS 7/6   GUESTS 10/-

March 31st: THE PEDDLERS

☆ THE REDCAR JAZZ CLUB ☆
COATHAM HOTEL   7 p.m.   THIS SUNDAY

FREE

PLUS

JUNCO PARTNERS

Guests 10/-

☆ THE REDCAR JAZZ CLUB ☆
COATHAM HOTEL   7 p.m.   THIS SUNDAY

JETHRO TULL

Plus "BLACK CAT BONES"

Members 7/6

10/-

FUTURE ATTRACTIONS

Sunday, August 23rd—**MOTT THE HOOPLE** ....plus — The Hammer

Sunday, August 30th—**TYRANNOSAURUS REX** .... plus — Karaelius

Monday, August 31st—**Y E S** ....**BRONCO**... Harvest Combine

Sunday, September 6th—**DUSTER BENNETT** .... SKID ROW

Sunday, September 13th—**BLODWYN PIG** ....plus — Super Eli

Sunday, September 20th—**F R E E** .... plus — Spyda

Sunday, September 27th—**BARCLAY JAMES HARVEST** .... URIA HEAP

Sunday, October 4th—**DERIK and the DOMINOS** — Eric Clapton, Jim Gordon, Carl Radle, Bobby Whitlock .... plus — Rivers Invitation

Tickets will be available for the following—Tyrannosaurus Rex, Yes, Blodwyn Pig, Free.
From—Hamiltons, Fearnleys, Calypso, Gentry.
Tickets for Derik and the Dominos available to members only from the club, price 20/- (from August 16th).

All Programmes are subject to alteration and the Committee cannot be held responsible for the non appearance of artists.

☆ THE REDCAR JAZZ CLUB ☆
COATHAM HOTEL   7 p.m.   THIS SUNDAY

BACK DOOR

PLUS

PRELUDE

Members 40p   Guests 60p

REDCAR JAZZ CLUB – INTRODUCTION

As I grew up in Teesside I devoured writing from my earliest days. Increasingly, I got into movies, theatre and visual art. As with most everyone, the television age pervaded so much though radio remained an abiding pleasure as well as somewhere I worked for a while.

All these were and remain stimuli for my work and some became vehicles for its publication, performance and transmission.

But my over-riding impression from those formative years is that while all of those cultural genres were hugely influential, Teesside was its music – no less for me.

The amount of home grown talent of my generation was simply exceptional. But it was also that those who visited and played at the venues we all frequented as though they meant it got taken to heart, a reception they'd remember and an experience that lived with them and made them return.

It's how you recall that 'fan' is derived from 'fanatic'.

Whilst I was working on this collection I was reminded of this by reading the excellent 'Backstage Pass – Redcar Jazz Club' by Dennis Weller, Chris Scott Wilson and Graham Lowe. For me, the Jazz Club on a Sunday evening was the venue.

There was always an extra, 'rite of passage' spice added as, at my age, I shouldn't have been able to get in. But hey, it's what you did....

The following piece was inspired by memories re-awoken by the book and is dedicated to the authors and all the performers, including those I wasn't able to mention in the poem.

REDCAR JAZZ CLUB

For Dennis Weller, Chris Scott Wilson, Graham Lowe and all the great performers

Lucky boy.
I was a child of
The Welfare State
The NHS and, best,
The '44 Education Act –
Free orange juice,
Tiny bottles of milk
Imbibed along with
A broadening
Of learning
And learning
Of broadening
– And
I was born with
Rock and roll

At my first gig
I saw The Shadows
And
'Stars Fell on Stockton'
So it felt, and with
Telstar and Tornados
Blowing me away on
My first 45s.
Otis Redding, R&B and
Beatles
On Ready, Steady, Go!
In technicolour black
And white.

By the time I
Found my way
To the fabled
Redcar Jazz Club
Rock and Prog
Was inheriting
The mantle

And I was ready
To take it on.

Sunday even song
At seven on the seafront
Until, leather-lathered
Turned out tipsy
With threat of tinnitus
To tomorrow's teaching
Was what I did
For denim congregation.
A pre-dogeared ticket
From Alan Fearnley's
Was my passport
Up the steep
Concrete stairway
To a kind of heaven
A dazzling
Dominion –

Met my mates on
Balcony over bar
Below,
By crate not bottle,
Beerbusy blokes bought
Brown Ale before
Bruised ballroom
Was blitzed
Into brilliance
By ear-bending
Electric excitement
And excellence –
To-be-stars, bars and
Air guitars

There are those
Who showed
The way to
New horizons
In my musical
Landscape;
Who kindled
A love that
Never left; and,
Made me think
About performance –
Live and raw –
Of what was felt,
What was meant
And invented.

I see the
Survivors still
Musicianship
Undiminished
Like my appreciation
And my debt.

My debut was Cream
In '67 as Jazz and Blues
Turned to rock
With Jack and Ginger
He was Ornette,
Slowhand and god
Then Eric was Derek
And Jack was Lifetime

Lead to
Mayall and Mark Almond
Gabriel Genesis, Rory G
Gentle Giant and Tull
Free, Fairports and
Green's
Fleetwood, Fairweather-
Lowe
Floyd for 7/- Money!

Yes and BJH – Nice;
Magificent precision
Invention and demand
For Fripp and Crimso
Kings then and now.

Back Door
Down from Blakey
Backing Colosseum
Soft Machine to
Matching Mole,
Bonzo Dog, Elkie Brooks
And pre-Zep Plant.

By now I was
Battling Bakelite switches
And big Marshall boxes
Into the back of
Battered Bedfords
For beer and a
Backstage pass.
Beginning and end

Though I
Reprised for Roxy
And Eno
In '72, my last
Blaze of glory a
Bonfire on the beach
After Curved Air in '71
(Sonja, oh Sonja)
And a door-opening
Exchange with Francis
Monkman
About keyboards

Waveforms
And tape loops

That turned me on
To Terry Riley;
In C and IN SEA.
With North Sea
Close to the East.

So, that night was
Not burning bridges
Or boats but
Building them
Beacon before beacon
Lit across
The landscape
Heartland to
Headland to
Higher ground
Signifying
'Moving on'
For broader and
Bigger
But never bettered,
I learned.

HAMBLETON HILLS FROM THE A19

For William Wordworth and Chris Rea

Dark and more dark
The shades of
Midwinter afternoon
Fell, deep
As I remember.

Christmas Eves
Driving 'home'.
Tees delta –
No blues;
Chris Rea draws
A smile with
His story song
Spot on
Radio repeats –
Familiarity with no
Contempt
Is the Yuletide Way –
Or the A19
Remarking Leake Hall,
Mount Grace and fall
Down
To The Tontine
As thousands tell
The tarmac tale
Drivedream

Across
Open country
Between
Full floods
Melting moon
Coined silver
In milky shallows

Of sweetwater sky
Clearing.
I wonder why
I see only
The shadowsnow
Shaped art
On those sleeping
Hills beyond
Silhouetted.

Look inward –
The lie of the land
When what I planned
Was the truth of my hand
As if I could reach out
From here and feel home
In your familiar contours;
Empty gestured

You accommodated me
Easily, all the while I try
To accommodate
You
Droveroaded too
Lines of least
Resistance
Joining points
William paced out

In reverie
Wordsworth walks
Above Osmotherley
Still striding, edge
Eyes distance
And wonders,
'Does she think
Of me
Still
As she seeks
Sleep.
And, waking,
Wander as I do.
Lonely?'

Teesside bluesman Chris Rea and the family firm!

Lyric –
Known and loved
And what I sense
Lies behind
Hill's sudden rise
Iceformed too
An age ago

Nearly Teesside
And 'Me Mam's'

> 'Dark and more dark the shades of evening fell;
> The wished for point was reached'
>
> From 'Composed After A Journey Across The Hambleton Hills'
> William Wordsworth

'William Wordsworth 1842' by Benjamin Robert Haydon. Haydon portrays a pensive, Romantic poet in a twilit hill landscape. I choose to place him on the Hambleton Hills where he did walk. digital image © 2020 National Portrait Gallery

BILSDALE BLUES

The deep
August air
Filled
Honeyed by bees
High on heath
Endeavour

On the tops
The livid moor
Bruised with heather
Bloom
Scorched earth
And aspiring
Green

Below
Butterflied
By vapour trails
Bilsdale blues.
Through the trees
Generous spread
And slide
Of subtle shade
Modified
And the fine
Weather whiteness
Of floatcloud
Over viscous valley;

Summer slowly
Climbed
The daleside
Opposing

Norsenames –
The road ribbons
From Wainstones
By Urra
Seave Green and
Chop Gate
To Helmsley.

Backroad driving
Before the Abbeys
I stop
Step out
And savour
The heat haze
Warping warm
Tarmac
The timely tick of
Motor cooling and
Sense of being
Submerged in
An ocean of air.

Scents and sounds
Of summer stills
My own noise
For a moment

I am open to
Changing characters
Against this background

Viewpoints

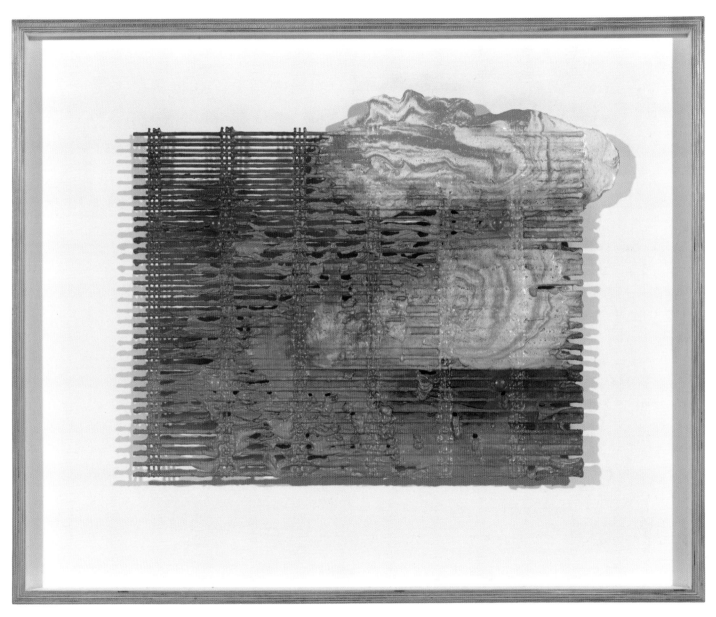

'The Helmsley Sky Studies – 9H' by William Tillyer © *2020 William Tillyer*

FROM BEHIND THE BLUE DOOR – HELMSLEY WALLED GARDEN

Pausing
To savour
The stillness
I heard
Their bright
Conversation
From behind
The blue door
No words
But cadence
And cascade,
Stresses and
Intonations –
Outdoor
Chamber music that
Spoke poems of
Castle, ditches
Baileyrock and
Planned parkland
Vistas opening
Outside this
Fecund and
Fruitful
Walled garden.
Abundance
By growing
Architecture, soft
Across the
Giving ground
Segmented and

Up its brick,
Wired and wicker
Walls.
All in its place
And proper.
Contrast; colours
Kaleidoscope
Changes at
Every turn
Of view and
Season
Eyefeasting

The deep
And fragrant
Mash of
Sun-induced smells
Savours
Like the produce
Was already
In pot or pie,
Pourri or preserve;
Petrichor where
Tender plantlets
Pressed into
Soft earth
Were watered

Composition

'Blue Door, White Chair' by J.P. Powls © 2020 J.P. Powls

DUSK – WALLED GARDEN FROM THE CASTLE THROUGH CROWN GLASS LEADED WINDOW

Slate blue
And stop-frame
Grey silence
Slow shadow
Fall
Over the green
Apple bruised
With beauty
Dusk garden
Blooms
Breezebrush
Blush And kiss
Breath held last
Brief blaze dims
Colour becomes
Shade for
Naked world
Innocent in love
Once more

With feeling;
Farewells
To forgotten
Days of devotion
Red rose
Romances
Sing out
Still secret

All stories
In walled dusk
Garden
Coloured
Into the blues
Of faded
Forget-me-nots

And Lavender
Tied there
Drying
In a posy
Picked partly
To obscure
The view

Pale petals
Of moon open;
To love,
Their light
Is absence
Beautifully distorted

My English heritage

'Dusk Garden Portrait' by Lindsay Mullen © *2020 Lindsay Mullen*

BIRCH HAGG WOOD – FARNDALE

For Lindsay Mullen

Hagg is spring

By
Dove and
Syke
Domain of daffodil
Eventide
Springrhymes
As April succeeds
March, marker May
Beckons
Birch,
Bluebell bud
As summer starts
To ease into
Place
And meadow
Gives way to
Coppice and copse
Weaves into wood
In goldgreen fury
To grow;
Rhythm of
Jazzdance
This passage
This movement
This stand

Adaptive Measures

'Adaptive Measures III' by Lindsay Mullen © 2020 Lindsay Mullen

FIRE DISPUTES THE COMMON GROUND – FARNDALE

For Peter M. Hicks

Deep summer;
What passes
Between us?
The sky has changed
Sun's burn
Obscured by smoke
On the horizon.
Those many desert days
Fevered hot
Tinder, brittle, snap;
Judgement fuels fires
No spontaneous combustion
Who knows where
The spark comes from;
Determination,
Distorting lens,
Dry storm lightning,
Discarded shard
Of something smashed,
Long smouldering ember
Of some fire before,
Not forgotten –
Some burning issue.
Driven breath
Compelled

In the heat
Of the moment
Fans the flame,
Blazing.

Consuming passion
Eats the air
Favours heat over light
Pursuing scorched
Earth policy –
Charred administration.

Does it die
Exhausted or
Quenched, resolved,
Healed by a
Changing sky?

Does it leave
New life
On learning
Earth
Or just choking ash
On barren waste
And fingers burned?

A distant hope

'Farndale, North Yorkshire Moors' by Peter M. Hicks © 2020 Peter M. Hicks

BLADERUNNER CONSTELLATION 2020

For Ridley Scott

A blazing night of no horizon
Vantage
High on Eston Hills
Nightridge, short of Nab
Where the ironstone founder
Makes his point
And matters are brought to a head,
The heavens below
C-beams glitter in the dark
Stacks, arcs and steady neon strewn
With careless intent;
Like myriad uncut gems,
Seamed from a rich vein,
Spread on the merchant's velvet.
It is a bladerunner constellation
In a chemical galaxy spiral
On a slagblack firmament.
It has its starburst flares
Spread supernova red, yellow
Then dark as the blackest hole
And the towering nebula steam
Colours changing definition
On the cooling, dense medium.

Expanding once, so fast
Yet too slow to see;
Now contracting
With only the memory
Of its molten birth,
Which, exploding, made
Its order from cracked chaos.
The cracked earth, dying
Of this magnificence.

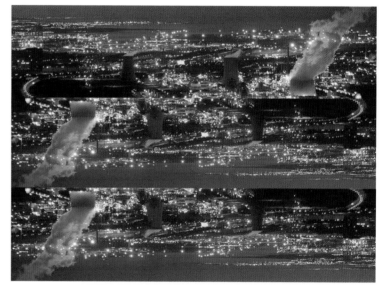

'Spinner Street Art' – Hill Street Centre car park
Image © 2020 Reach Plc with permission from Teeside Live

PATHS

For Robert Macfarlane – Poet and, in my view, the outstanding
contemporary writer on English landscape and language

Paths are customs
Of landscape –
Habit marks
Of man and nature
Ingrained over time
By many
From new ground
Broken by one
And only then
Immediately obvious
To agreeing feet.
Slowly, surely,
Care worn or
Carelessly
Deliberate,
Felt underfoot –
Archive of steps
The way
To a place
Becomes itself
A place
Of experience
And meanings, not
To be missed –
Learning.
Least resistance
Lines up
For discipline, chosen –

Rabbit run to
Sheep trod to
Footpath to
Holloway to
Highway and
Byway by way
Of being memorial
To time immemorial.
The moment
Stretched.

Like thought
Folded in
On itself,
Hedgewall
Tree tunnel
Lazy lane laden
With blossom or
Berries; closebound.
Ahead
The drawing path
Curves
Into the beyond

For the undiscovered
Country
Life is the placemaker

Free to roam
Own your own
All directions
Home

There and back
Again;
Lost words
Recovered
Living poems
Discovered

AYRESOME PARK AND THE RIVERSIDE STADIUM

The debates about the religious, astronomical, horological and agricultural purposes of Stonehenge continue.

But, any football fan approaching Avebury stone circle, its near neighbour in the Neolithic landscape, from the South-East via its impressive West Kennet Avenue of stones, knows in their heart and guts that it's an arena.

Nightlit by the guttering flames of a thousand brushwood torches and bankpacked with a rowdy, partisan crowd it would have had quite the atmosphere. It can be felt still. It is step-hurrying special to approach.

So it is with some football grounds – here is Anthony Vickers unearthing the 'archeological' essence of Middlesbrough FC's previous home before they moved to The Riverside Stadium twenty-five years ago.

'Ayresome was a powerful cultural symbol and central to the Teesside psyche, the focus for shared experience handed down through the years, the dad-and-lad rite-of-passage of first love that blossomed into an intense if not always fulfilling life-long passion and duty.

Ayresome Park was the physical representation of our history, our identity; it was the last resting place of dashed hopes and broken dreams piled up a century deep.

But it was also the venue for great moments of pride and joy and hope and vivid memories echoed down the years. There may not have been a lot of success but there was a lot of history.'

Four generations of my family have held that expectancy-over-experience inheritance through most of that history and beyond – and we're planning on a fifth! It's always the hope that gets you.

The move to The Riverside brought more success to the team and, pleasingly, the following has become much more diverse. But the ride is still roller-coaster as that venue builds its own landscape layers of legend and builds character and characters.

The Boro football grounds were and are the beating heart of the town. People walk taller when their team is doing well – they never walk alone. And nights under lights are still step-hurrying special...

'Hurry Up, Or We'll Be Late' by Philip Meadows © 2020 Philip Meadows

NIGHTS UNDER LIGHTS

For Philip Meadows and Anthony Vickers

Tucked into
Tightly packed terraces
Or sitting spacious,
Middle havened
With flyover, underpass,
Railway and dock;
Pathe News past
HD 4G present;
Giz a squeeze gate
Season card swipe;
Bovril or beer;
Nana knitted
Bobble hat or
Branded
Baseball cap;
Power Game or
Pigbag;
At heart
It's all the same
It's in the blood.

Join ever-growing
Gathering flow of
Moist-eyed, radged
Grey gadges,
Families and friends,
Lads and Dads,
'Me, like'
Wide eyed zealots
Common cause
Fellow fans follow
Common causeway
To set apart isle
Of haloed green
Midst cloaking tide
Of midweek dark.
Chummy caustic
Chatter, cliches
Polished to a shine
Nuggets of truth
Unearthed and
Rehearsed.

Talk turned tribal.
Not 'fond' or
'Touched', Pet –
Potency of the
Still possible.
Small, signal icons,
Age old habits
And match day
Rituals and routes
Lead to legion
Of legends
Floodlit field
Of hopes and fears
Down all these years.
The home ground

Step-hurrying
Glow in the sky,
Mirroring many
A mazy run
Of the mind;

Something stirring
In the night air;
Sudden shouts;
Swelling songs
Swirling;
Accents, aromas,
Aptronyms abound;
Long before
Contours of the
Processional ways
Determine to
Allow catch of
First sight of
Gathering place
Wreathed in light
For the faithful
Wrapped in red.
Sky at night.
And always the
Catch of breath.

'Smoggies and Proud' by *Philip Meadows* © 2020 Philip Meadows

RED 2

Green between
Holgate and Bob End
Is terrace and turnstile
Bloodmemory;
Now temenos
Landscape, composed,
For purpose
In performance
All set to ignite
On riverside site.

Colours colonise
Like the opening bars
Of an anthem
Keylit by late
Summer sun
Slipping slowly
Below stand
Provides fanfare;
When tribute sounds,
It is as though
'Red' was newly
Discovered
And a definition
Was needed;

Pitch perfect
Before season
Segues to its
Themes, motifs
And harmonies
With a glory

All their own

Minted new

Clear, the
Steel river
Reflects
On winter's song
Suggested
Red too
And, molten, calls
To suites of spring

Our transporter

'Temenos and Transporter' by Lynne@SmoggieArt
© 2020 SmoggieArt

Riverside brick by John Powls
© 2020 John Powls

'Ayresome Park' by Lynne@SmoggieArt © *2020 SmoggieArt*

NORTHERN LIGHTS – IT'S THE HOPE THAT GETS YOU

For Ali Brownlee

Distant
Eston Hills
Have found
The service
Of clouds
Refusing
Any penetration of
Unsuccessful sunlight
Slight suitor
Weak oblique
Unwanted;
Under cover
Surrendered to
Rhythm and rests
Rain drumming
Drenching noise
Muffled ground
Sodden green
And trodden brown
Wet desert
Unsatisfied

Drenched
Riverside rain
Falls hard
To impatient
Stand and pitch
Underfoot
Sodden trodden
Programme promises
Rejected shadow
Floodlights play
LED and neon arc
Girds stadium
Whetted whiteglow
Improbable reds
Pulse galvanic
'Everybody round my
House for a Parmo!'
Can't be. Again?!
Drumming hardbeat
Wet desert
Satisfied

Images © 2020 Reach Plc with permission from Teeside Live

'The Riverside Stadium' by Lynne@SmoggieArt © *2020 SmoggieArt*

'Teesside Aerial Landscape Image' by David Bell © *2020 David Bell*

INTERPONTES – BETWEEN THE BRIDGES

For David Bell

Daystars rise;
That dawning says
'We shall be'

Slow outlines sense,
Watermarked in
Waiting page

All children
Of the once
Infant Hercules

Up for the
Challenge of
Broadening day

Uncontained –
Between the bridges
The borders of

Myths, legend,
Hard fact are
Not yet decisive

Comes the breath
Of aspiration
And imagination

To sweep the air
Build invention;
A clearer picture

To reveal them
At the nub
Of things again

Reborn to deed
Eloquence – doers
Dawn to dusk.

'Middlesbrough Art Gallery II, Evening' by Andrew Gifford © *2020 Andrew Gifford. Image credit MIMA*

'Linthorpe Road South, Night II' by Andrew Gifford © *2020 Andrew Gifford. Image credit MIMA*

LINTHORPE ROAD – IN THREE MOVEMENTS

For Andrew Gifford

i

The line
Of poetry
Stretches
To and through
The landscape
To which all
Poets come
Eventually
An abstraction
Into words
Our true colours;
At ground,
Molten blue,
Rough-ruched velvet,
Lapis stream
Liquid aesthetic flows
With the logic
Of a dream;
A transport for
Imaginings.
Strung out strands
Of rainbows drip
With shades;
Wine and tar
Opal blood
Fig ripening cut
Grain rinsed husk
Ice candy and
Funk punk rouge
Run together.

Stop. Punctuates.
A moment
Falls open,
Frame by frame,
Revealing, ripe
A more shapely chaos.
Street sussurus
Aluminium cloud,
Sky control,
Intrusive cobalt

ii

**There's a long
Road running**
From The Village
To The Town
From Roman road
To the ford
From Roman Road
To Boho and River
Straight in
To stories, rising
Remembrances
Time and space
Travellers' tales
Meaning and memories
A wayfarer's weave
Got with walking –
That time, this time
Next time; who
What, where, when –

Some of those semi-
Honest servers
Windowshop hardware
Of happenings store.
And sometimes, why?
That restaurant,
Those shops,
This museum,
That home, pub, park
Or cinema caught
In the glowing dark;
Slick dark slabs
Paving my way
Lustred by wet
With lamptrails
Ribboning road
As if set by moving
Moonlight purpose
On slow surface of
A river of
Reflection

iii

Under gentle drench
Blackblue roofs
Pitched shining
Reclining;
Light caught
In heavy lidded
Yellow-white
Windows.

Talking pictures.
Under streetlamp
Sodium skyspilt
Evening unscrolls
And headlight flow
Hard and tender
In that vein
Embracing fierceness
Soft rain
Slowfalls from
Velvet wrapped
Sky
Simplifies issues
As day wanes
And drains
Rain on panes;
Droplets dance
Perform physics;
Glass, darkly
Screens designs;
Slow red and amber
Black tarmac shine
Colour of lost love
Reflected in gutters
Rainbows run with
Signs of neon
In passing, **Evening Crawl**
Disorderly mix
Town to village
The journey home;
Appetite whetted
By daily grindstone

'Linthorpe Road Line Painting II' by Andrew Gifford © 2020 Andrew Gifford. Image credit MIMA

SUPERMOON OVER SALTBURN PIER WITH COMET CODA

For Kevin Forth and for super Saltburn

Weight of water
Wait of water
Tips the balance
Of power
For the cliff lift
That spills out
Its draught
To its companion
And completer
Pier balanced
Straight standing
Over the waves
On their
Moonpulled
Advance
And retreat
Balanced low
On the Saltburn
Skysea
Is yearfirst full
Supermoon
Howlwolf held
Cloudmaster holds
The gaping skies
Apart

Loving the blue
Silence
On reflection

Thoughts
Caught in
Wavebreak white
And shining clear
Like giltamber
Wolfeye images
Placed by
Moonlight purpose
On the surface
Of the sea –
Measuring
The limit of
Iron ambition
Balanced

I ask
Quiet questions
Of the icemoon
January warm
As it still
Spins and weaves
This brilliant night

Huntcliff watches,
Its own age-old
Balance to strike
With three-tailed traveller
Against stardusted
July sky.

'Supermoon over Saltburn Pier'
by Kevin Forth © 2020 Kevin Forth

'Comet Neowise over Saltburn Pier'
by Kevin Forth © 2020 Kevin Forth

'IN SEA'

North Sea To The East *recognises the significance of seascape to Teesside and North Yorkshire as well as their landscape. 'IN SEA' celebrates that seascape in a very particular way.*

I have long appreciated and been inspired by the work of internationally renowned composer Terry Riley. In 1964 Terry composed a seminal work which he titled 'In C'.

Using a structural reference point drawn from 'In C' and Terry's pioneering ways of working I developed a grid set of 53 five line poems, styled 'poettes', inspired by seascape and coastline and titled 'IN SEA'.

I continue to develop the piece, exploring its variations and possibilities. I have recorded several versions of 'IN SEA' which are available through my YouTube channel which is easily accessed via the 'IN SEA' page on my website www.promiselandpoetry.co.uk

The version of the poem that appears herein is one of those variations and was developed alongside the beautiful paintings of Kay Spare produced in an iterative exchange over several months in 2020.

> *'John, I am happy that my work has been meaningful for you. Thanks for sharing this poem with me. It is great. It must be exciting to hear it read by different performers.'*
> > *Terry Riley*

All the paintings on pages 86 and 87 are by Kay Spare

'Pearl Mother Pink'

'After the Tempest'

'Silver Light'

'Seas' Many Tongues II'

'Soon the Moon'

'Wine Dark Seas'

'A Grey Gouache'

'I Fell in Love II'

'The Sea Light II'

'Rivage III'

'Darkening Sky'

'Rivage I'

'Light Fantastic IV'

'Lights Across the Bay'

'Light Fantastic II'

A cubist view
Of the North
Sea to the East
in 53 poettes

In Sea, In Sea a
Ceaseless peace
Of wonder; In Sea
In Sea a ceaseless
Piece of wonder

The waves surge
Dark and supple
Crashing oils laid
By bright slashing
Palette knife

A grey gouache
Of scoured sky
Drizzling to a flat
Calm and empty
Seascape; waiting

Foaming, breaking
Wild successions
Salted sequences
Crashing climaxes
Brush with spirit

Questionable
Shore - status of
Seas open
Weather and way;
My small soul

Refuge and
Prospect,
Harbour and
Horizon; open
Breakwater arms

Navigator, wayfarer
Storytrader, leader;
Susceptible to their
Beauty and stories
Begin and end here

At each cut in cliff
Where streams sea
Selves a-tumble of
Red tile rooves run
Spilldown to staithes

Set above stones
Forever and for
The better, turn
Impression of
Light permanent

Salt water has
A long memory –
Things it learned
From moonwinds
Imaginings wake

Open breakwater
Arms gathering
Waves calming
In sanctuary stave
Anchored cobles

Beaten bronze
Sand channeling
Quicksilver water
A cause way
A causeway

The grammar of
Land and sea
Has the poignancy
Of music; muses
Of memory

Sand, strand, shelf,
Cliff, dune, groyne,
Breakwater, scar,
Bay, point and gare
Map character

I was born and
Raised with sea
Close to the East
I recognise coasts
Redeemer – akin

Weight of water
Wait of water
Released by river
And tide collide
Monumental made

The sealight lifts
And sifts through
Mists to expose
The great mirror
Of the skies still

Sudden deep rush
Black and beautiful
Starless and cold
Moonfree slick across
Slack water's run

The sand stained
Vagabond strand
The wrack and roll
Of breakers crash
And tow foaming

Haar holds cold
And close washes
The quiet scene
Between tide turns
To watercolour

Seas' many
Tongues translate
To conversations;
Surfwords swell
On meeting land

Experience moves
Beyond elemental
Soliloquies primal
Transactions of
A living Earth

Air to water catch
Lightning fast in
Stained glass bottle
Sea silkslow show
Kaleidoscopes know

The dying gold
Bequeathed
Molten tribute
To the waters
Stirring quench

Wordbringer trade
Winds wash hoards
Of meaning with
Each wave from
North and East

Water relic –
Wavewash over
Sand dissolve and
Remake with each
Moonpulse move

Spindrift haze
Windwhipped from
Breakers' crests
Fleet rainbows
From slanting sun

Made new slate
Broken sandstone
Where waves run
Drain and break
Made clean slate

Scent of sea
Windborne warm
Frets onto shore
To dew the moors
With cool jewels

Ocean arc meets
Rocks and strand
High tide mark of
Expression, solid
Founded, meeting

Windowwatch
Time and tide
Waiting though
They will not; slow
Love relentless

This is a sea that
Rhymes with sky
This is the air with
Rhythms of water
Blue wash dreams

Huntcliff to Westcliff
The seasun time
Gliterpath lambent
At edge of things
Daylong gnomon

Wine dark seas
Draw you and me
Undertow, so flow
Willingly pulled to
Our wild odyssey

The river rushes
To spend itself
In sea – estuary
Is negotiable
Boundary treaty

Lighthoused
The long pulse
Of light; seeming
Quickened when
The fog bell tolls

The sea light more
Than physics
More than meets
The eye – behold
Illumination made

Sea fastened
Restless moon
Seeks dawn's
Release from
Moving waters

Beachcombing
Sunset shells
Sound the sea
Stroking shore
Pearlmother pink

Haar and fret mists
So loyal to this
Sealand they were
Named even for
Beauty obscured

Soon the moon
Makes grace trail
Of molten silver
Across the sea
It moves; poetry

Lone rapture -
The experience
Of seascape
Thinking time
Breathing space

All too easily
I am drawn into
Its deep dominion
Of dreams and
Desiring; waving

Shore lines, signs
Of storms tensing
To force horizon
Apart. Rent
Elemental – torn

Feel the soft swell
Roll to horizon
And beyond;
Sea's reach
Intimate power

Violently neutral,
Unstudied in its
Indifference; great
Slabs of grey, cold
Impassive volumes

Tides turn
Transitory and
Fugitive – suggest
As they expose
And secrete

No vague skies
No ordinary cloud
No throwaway
Lines - straight to
The point. Bay

Great birdstore
Frees wheeling
Sing and surge in
White waves
Over reef rocks

Waverider
Stormbreaker
The rock adamant
Stands the test
Of timetide beside

The soft machine
Sociable surface
Hidden depths
Whetstones mark
Narrow courses

Blank presence
Colour from none
Constant changing
Immerse, isolate
Or against nature

In Sea, In Sea a
Ceaseless peace
Of wonder; In Sea
In Sea a ceaseless
Piece of wonder

IN SEA
For Terry Riley
and 'In C'

TEESMOUTH

TO

ESKMOUTH

The sea is all about us

'Sea and Sky' by J.M.W. Turner Turner Bequest, Tate Britain; digital photo © 2020 Tate

SEA AND SKY – UNFOLDING LIGHT

For Baldr and the Daughters of Ran

The sublime
Committed
To paper
Abstraction
Where the light
Suffuses
Slow through
Lucent
Lapis plush
Edge of blue

Salty indifference
Skyground bound
Heavens,
Stormdark light
Coaljet bright,
Parted
Revealing its
Fleeting lineage

Raw page emptied
Canvas coloured
Calm before

Icon
Almond glow
Where arcs
Of seaskin and sky
Intersect new
Bluerain horizons
Meniscus

Implied

Correspondence.
The consolation
Of land
Intimate, known,
Dependents contention
Comparing mythologies

Words untethered
Unfurl and flex
Themselves
Lyric
With space to
Drift and grow
And time hangs
Loosely
Deep and dreamless

Dimensions
A moving theatre
For weather
Writhing above
The wild, blue
Wavemusic
Carrying a voice
Soaring,
The chorus of light
The sing of shore
In ecstasies

A soft unfolding
Light
Seeming solid
Fills the frame
Mirrored
Air in rounds
Foaming
Raw white silk
Drawn over supple
And beaten silver
Like precious pale
Moon tidetied
At each new dawn
Fixed

For just this moment

'Kettleness Scar VIII' by Kay Spare © *2020 Kay Spare*

HARVEST PERSPECTIVES

For Kay Spare

Harvest heads above
Harvests from the deeps
Of land and sea
All in their seasons
Currency.

From the point
Kettle Ness Scar
Telltale leachblue wash
Alum veined flow below
Bruisestripe of heather
Succeeding gorse's
Outrageous flowering
Of Spring sun
Hiding the black
Polished to poets'
Stone; salt water
Cured treecarbon
Jet unearthed

From its alumrhyme
Bluegrey fastnesses
Where waves break
The rock fingers
Reach and rake
Fray the sea
Fleet clouds and salt
Kiss breeze blown
Feel all is provisional
Ion charged positive
With possibilities

To and from the waters
Like stone rails
On a staithe
Where the cliff was
Hauled up, bluff;
Silvercatch

From field; boundary
Seasky glow, salt radiant
Shines undefined
Somewhere behind
Where land slips
Sharp away: flats

Foregrounds
Palette knife
Constable corn, goldstruck
Brushborn of sun
Next field of barley
Nod heads and sway
Saturated in specific
Shades of our setting
Star in their ripetime
Soaked in amber
Honey sulphur straw
Saffron cadmium
Chrome lemon
Light promise

From
The Cleveland Way

93

'Nod Heads and Sway' by Richard Spare © *2020 Richard Spare*

'Kettleness Scar VII' by Kay Spare © *2020 Kay Spare*

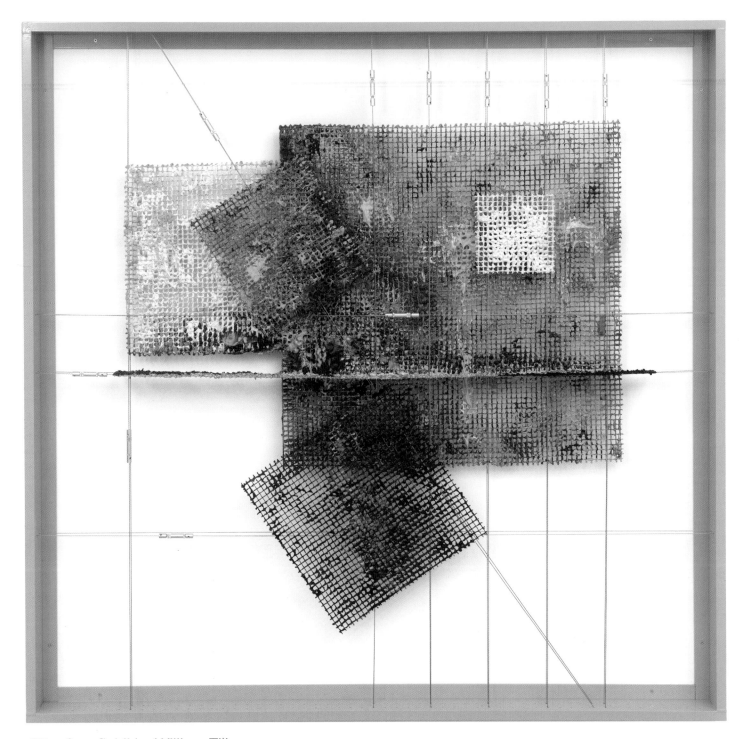

'The Cornfield' by William Tillyer © *2020 William Tillyer*

96

WORKS

Driven
Discipline
Of clouds
Constable
Caught

Frame   Cornfield   Mettle
Shown
Line drawn   Planes

Mulgrave
Tensile
Wire works
Landscape
August taut

SANDSEND

For Ian Mitchell

Walking
All along
The beach
On a day
That started
So grey
It was brown
But, seaward,
Sunclearing;
Sullen art, lifting
Shifting –
The strand,
The sand packed,
The wrack
And roll
Of North Sea breakers
And the brackish stream
Seeking rough sanctuary
From saturated moor.

Its mood
And magnificence
Captured
To share with you
For its promise
And its bearing
Under the weight
Of history

Myth and legend –
Harbouring
Without wound; words
This love of
Time and tide
This northland –
Bodily, boldly
In broadening
Daylight
Endlessly.
Can you tell too?

'Sandsend Beach' by Ian Mitchell © *2020 Ian Mitchell*

WHITBY

'*Surf Sequence – Whitby*'
by Carol Ballenger
© *2020 Google/Tera Metrics*

'Distant View of Whitby from the Moors' by J.M.W. Turner Turner Bequest, Tate Britain; digital photo © 2020 Tate

THE RITUAL ROUTE – WHITBY INCANTATION IN TEN PARTS

For Aman Ral-Powls to whose empty chair next to mine I've recited this after each visit to Whitby
so his memory might know too

Whitby is quintessential –
Real and reliable;
Nostalgia and now
And to come.
This is its essence
For me.

Ritual begins
Before Route
First sight of
Sun spotlit
Abbey always,
From Moor road
Near Ugthorpe

What's good enough
For J.M.W. Turner...

Almost where
'Four mile glide' began –
Except for one
Fixed-wheel fanatic –
When Dad and mates
Cycled it
Just after the War.

I

Station Square,
Trains steam
Endeavour Wharf and
Broadbeam bark replica

Along New Quay then
Up steep bank to
Flowergate
Goth garlanded

Cappuccino and scones
At Sherlock's cafe
'Cheese for me
If they've got them'
A good 7.5 on
The Sconometer.
Skinner Street, Belle Vue
Due North for Westcliff.

II

Royal Crescent
No appetite to bite
On Mrs. Veazey's
At blue plaqued No. 6
(Theatricals welcome)
Bram Stoker lodged
As did the novel idea
For Dracula with him
While he walked
Writers' town routes
In search of stories
Like Gaskell
And Carroll,
Dickens and Collins.
Gift for gift.

III

Line up whale's jawbones,
For rich resonance
With admired Abbey
Window arch away
Across the harbour.

Statue earned
Engagement
Ambivalence around
Cook –
Still a hero –
And celebration of whaling.
Of their time?

IV

Steep steps steady
To Khyber Pass.
S down and round
Along breakwater pier.
Reach restored lighthouse
No longer light
Or house, of course.

State of sea,
Tide and wavebreak
White horses.
On a perfect day
Only sea and wind –
Fleet clouds and salt kiss,
Breeze blown.

All is provisional
But ion charged
With possibilities.

Promenade quayside
By fish market
Takeaway troughers tangle
With ginormous gulls
Gigging as gannets
Gorging, both.

V

Fresh and salty fellows
Flowing below,
Human tides collide
On either side
Of swing bridge;
Flows only stemmed
Paradoxically
By occasional closures
Caused by its opening.

Ad hoc audience
Assembles
For top harbour traffic,
However mundane.

All the while, polar bear,
Frozen on patrol, wisely
Keeps his cool counsel.

VI

Sandgate's squeeze
Threads to market square.
Thwarted-before-it-begins
Search to spot
Traditional deep blue,
Rope and ladder gansey
In shop windows.

But everywhere,
Whitby jet.
Semi-precious,
Site specific, Goth-popular,
Alum partnering, polished,
Pressure hardened,
Brine cured, black
Monkeypuzzle-carbon
Victoriana, that is –
Not Whittle's
Whizzing progeny.

Church Street,
Old chapel steps;
Pause to pick out
Ghaut
Opposite – gunnel
With stone stair down
To the river at its end.
Hindi name, echoes
Sub-continent sailors

Of centuries past
Longing for long left
Equivalents on banks
Of sacred Ganges.

VII

199 Steps to the Abbey
Rising to the heights
Of Hild and Caedmon
Priestess princess and
Shepherd poet.

Hie to Henrietta Street
Rental cottage rows
Kipper smokehouse.
Rich and ripe
Oaksmoulder smells
Pervade but it's
'In principle'
over purchase.

Where path peters out
The prospect takes over
Quiet reflection on where
We've come from –
On our part

VIII

Retrace steps
Flagging on flagstones.

Back over swing bridge
But this time, cross
Into Baxtergate –
Botham's Brack –
Delicious detour.

IX

Station Square
Sniff the finishing
Straight and salivate
As temptation turns to
Deep fried gratification.

Sporting a steaming shoal
Of fish and chip eateries,
The Valhalla of victory
Is Trenchers
Quayside paean of
Fish Frier's art.
How long the queue?
It's worth it
And so are you!

Survivor of inundation
Usurper sea and Esk
Tidestole space together
Spinning salty seafarer
Stories. Silt settled as
Sail-road slipped
Back to its banks.

Haughty steam trains
Huffed
And stayed above
Trenchers rose renewed
Whitby essence
For me
Life goes on –
Battered
But unbowed;
Better
And blooming.

X

So, it comes full circle –
Just like one's belt
Now doesn't!

Rolling out replete,
Ritual Routed,
Ready to repeat
Already

But
Ready we now are
For ritual
To re-introduce
Bucket and spade
Amusements and rides
Rock and candy floss
Sand and rock pool
So, it comes full circle
Again

This page and opposite: 'The Ritual Route – Whitby' by Carol Ballenger © 2020 Google

WHITBY ABBEY – STREANESHEALH

For Janina Ramirez

The princess priestess
And the poet –
Their foundation
And eminence here.
In the very stones
A building's bones
That are grown to grace
The landscape;
Sitting proud
Of cliff, lea and pond,
A sanctity
Of work and nature
A flight
Of solid imagination
On the edge

Arch
Call and response
With West Cliff
Whalebones
Echoes over gothic,
Ghaut and ginnel
Under the gaze of
Navigator and novelist
Our ritual route
Marked out –
Both banks of Esk.

The sea
Subject
Only in words
Even with stone
Arms embrace
And jet black –
We celebrate endeavour
In town
Of transformations

Down through ages
Hild and Caedmon
Reason and rhyme
Shepherd still –
A certain spirit
Gathering voices

A small eternity

Whitby 17/125 *Norman Ackroyd* 2015

'Whitby' by Norman Ackroyd CBE, RA © 2020 Norman Ackroyd

MRS. ENDEAVOUR

For James Cook

The compass oak
Stood for justice,
Proud of the North
Yorkshire sward;
Acorn in the
Civil War,
Six score years of
Late to leaf
Late to fall –
Its own empire
With a different
Perspective on time,
Landscape's
Stories mapped
In every tight
Ring repository
For all encountered;
To stand alone;
Felled in prime.

Heartwood
Heart of oak
Pegged, nailed
And jointed
For the bark
Broad of beam

Fishburn's
Whitby Collier,
Mrs Endeavour –
Like their sounds,
Joiner of trees and sea
With two wisdoms –
For now
Seascape's stories
To map
Bearing her
Right name.
Voyaging, bound
For botany
Recorded in
Its gall ink
Immemorial
Though her time came
Repository
For all encountered;
To stand alone;
Scuttled in prime.

Charting
A life
Of exception;
The world over –

Marton to Ayton to
Staithes;
Whitby to Kealakekula.
Endeavour
And Resolution
From stoic Elizabeth
And shade children.
No clean geography
Not just
Your course
Being charted
Not just
Venus in transit
That was the way
Of the world –
Plotting.
Explorer, cartographer
Navigator, seamanship –
Unequalled.
Captain? My Captain
Can history
Ever be told
Without inevitably?
Unfold colonialism
Without consequence?
Chronos, your friend
But time's passed

Could atlas bear
That weight?
Maps, memorials,
Many named
Repository
For all encountered;
To stand alone;
Felled in prime

Fatefully,
Oak, collier, Cook –
Robust, purposeful
Calm, deliberate
Ordered, handsome
Steady, steadfast
Joined
As embodiments
Of the word

Endeavour.

'Whitby' by J.M.W. Turner *Turner Bequest, Tate Britain; digital photo © 2020 Tate*

AND PICKERING... AND MIDDLESBROUGH –
RAILWAYS OF THE NORTH YORKS MOORS TO AND FROM WHITBY TOWN

Trains of thought
Endless responses
Departing trains

Whitby and Pickering
61264 –
Return on Repton;
Alighting at Goathland
And returning to Grosmont
Walking the footpath
By the Murk Esk

Ribbons of
River and path
Lightly braid
Together
Bridges made
Works of translation

Woods
Pillared by sunbeams
Light through leaves
Slanting, sliding
Splashing into streams
Slipping sidelong into
The gleaming surface
Of a shadowed river
The glow of flowing
Water sprinkled
With shards of light

Sundered sunminted coins
Arcs and jagged edges
Glint and glide;
In passing
Murmurs music;
Splashdrop pearls
Pendant the tips
Of low lime leaves
Pointing up their
Heart shape simply
Made for holding
Jewels like this

Nature's source
Of art is love;
The heart
Watches and
Receives

Reboarding
At Grosmont
We stoked
Our way to
Whitby on 75029
The Green Knight
Flying proud pennons
Of smoke and steam
As Ruswarp, Sleights
And viaduct high whistle by.

Just who chose
To juxtapose
One of the world's
Loveliest lines
With the world's
Most unlovely
Diesel bustrains?
Inside and outside
Is a stark contrast
Starting with the
Gothic revival
Tiled ticket hall
Of Middlesbrough
Station like the great
Hall of a thane
Long gone and the
Perfect posters
Of Mackenzie Thorpe
Galleried.

Esk Valley braided
Rail and road
Over and under
And through
Two strand steel thread
It weaves strings for
A set of pearls
With trainrhythm names
Great Ayton, Battersby
Kildale, Commondale

Castleton, Danby, Lealholm
Glaisdale, Egton, Grosmont
Westcliff and Whitby Town

Patterned with
Irregular
Stonewall geometry
Greenskirts
With white dots
Gird the lower
Slopes of dales
Darktopped
By heatherburn

Once among ling
On the hill
Learning
The language
Of the wind
And the hover
A voice for
The voiceless
Two tone and track

Such scant summer
Service
Bookending beautiful days

Trains of thought
Endless responses
Departing trains

Above: '75029 The Green Knight at Grosmont' Below: 'The Esk Valley Line near Box Hall' both by Dr. Phil Brown
© 2020 Dr. Phil Brown

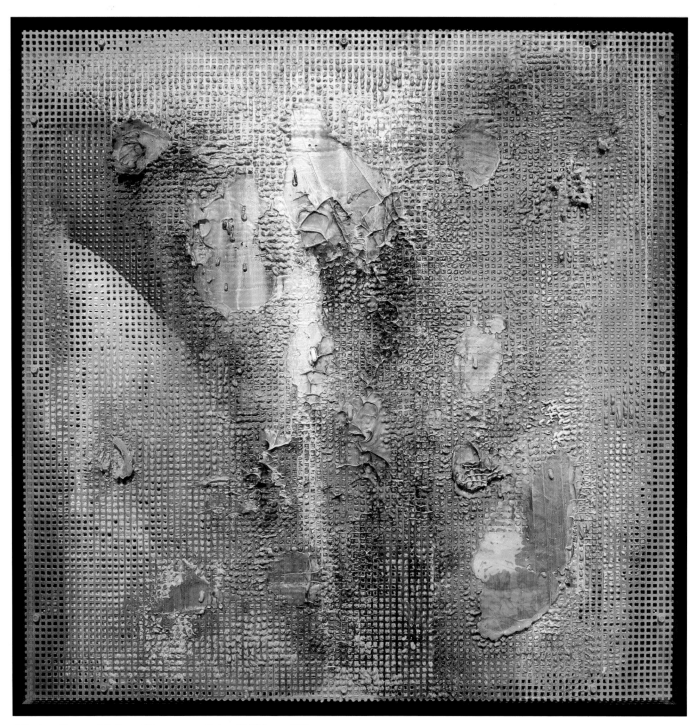

'Relentless: Esk – Grosmont' by William Tillyer © 2020 William Tillyer

FIRSTGREEN MURK ESK

For William Tillyer

Firstgreen
Golden light
Filtered through
New leaves
Host
Unfolding

Budyoung

Trumpets
An almost love
Song
To the sky
Tall
Very clear
Bluewarm

The wind brings
Tidings
And carries
The message
Growing
Through ages

The spirit
Of trees
In number

CASTLETON RIGG

For Judith

The seated man
Has moved on.
Over Westerdale
And Danbydale
Towards the source
Of the Esk;
Heatherblackened,
Brownbracken bare
Sheeptrod paths.
Fat Betty and
Young Ralph, stonestill,
Watch the winter sky
Slide indifferent,
Slowly down
Chromatic scales.
Reduce the tones
To glacier blue and
A long and sonorous
Umbral charcoal;
Diminuendo.

Three dimensions
Become two,
Lime ridge silhouette.
The last rooks, distant;
Cursive, inked characters
Moving, calligraphic,

Across and down
The blue page
Emptied.

Mood and landscape,
Defining times of peace
When even our own noise
Stills
For a moment.

Silence is a yardstick
By which other things
Are measured.

The vast structures
Of recollection.

Ways found.

'The Seated Man' by Sean Henry
photos © 2020 Judith A. Powls

ONOMASTICON – POETRY OF NAMING

Names that ring
Like iron on stone
Taste on the tongue
With the tang
Of salt spray
From North Sea
To the East
Make the hewn and
Windaged landscape
Where farm gives
Way to fell
Stern, wild and soft
Rainwracked
Rinsed of colour
Rumble with rhythms
Of Norse
And Old English;
Burning like
The furnace sky
Now sunset
Not smelter

Nappa Scar;
Kield Heads, Thowker,
Apedale Beck,
Reeth.
Booze, Whaw, Heelaugh,
Stang Top, Raw Bank,

Low Row, Crackpot,
Gunnerside,
Blades.
Satron Ivelet
Oxnop Ghyll, Wain Wath
Muker, Thwaite,
Keld.
Skeugh Head, Angram,
Stonesdale, Tan Hill
Buttertubs.
Foss Dale, High Shaw
Sedbusk, Hardraw
Appersett,
Hawes.
Gayle, Gearstones
Snaizeholme, Semer Water,
Countersett, Stalling Busk
Burtersett, Bainbridge
Askrigg.
Cubick, Thornton Rust,
Aysgarth.
Swinithwaite, West Witton,
Carperby, Bolton,
Redmire.
Sissy Bank, Scarth Nick,
Wensley, Whipperdale
Shawl Ridge,
Leyburn.

Names planted
Rooted
Firm and fruitful
Grafted
On stock of
Growing vigour
Cluster in groves,
Flocking fields
Fragrancing
Hay-meadow
Eyebright and clover
Endless boundaries
Settling
On successions
Of maps contouring
Our onomasticon
Hard, simple, natural
Cultivated, grown
Cropped
And the glint
Of a low sun
Framing my wordworld
Until this day.

'Dry Stone' by Mark Sofilas © 2020 Mark Sofilas

THE WORKINGS

For Mark Sofilas and Carol Ballenger

Filling
The hungry void
Airy and violent
Born drenchers
Hardrain drops
That thudded
On pillow peat
And sprung green
Sweetening
Leave as quickly
As they came.
Now fast shadows
Ripple
Bright and black
Over oreworked hills –
Drift, spoil and gallery
Scarcloaked.
Low on their flanks,
Stone and wood,
Tile and iron
Impermanence
Stand against
Sheering light
And driven water.
Hard by, their broken
Echoes remind.

Above
By sheeptrod way
The high grazing
Defined;
Greysnaking dry
Stonewalling
Squaring up

Holding ground
In elemental
Dispute;
Defending fields –
Territory held
For today;
How hardbright
That light falls
And runnels rush –
It's a view – but
Daleslife insists on
A hard domestic
Reading of the day

'Glyphs – Gunnerside Gill' by John Powls © 2020 Google Earth

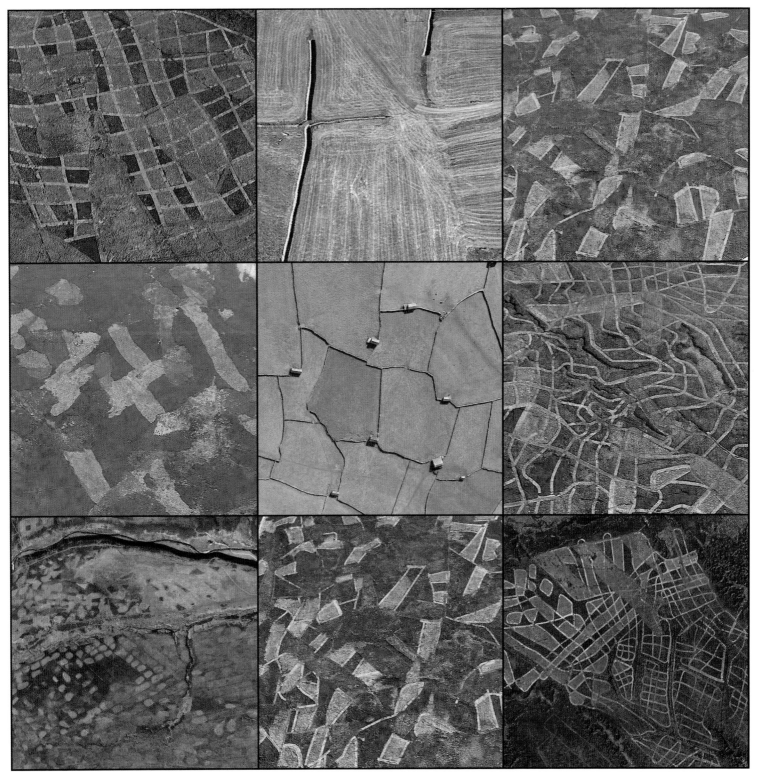

'Land Marks – Gunnerside' by Carol Ballenger © 2020 Google/CNES/Airbus

'Gunnerside' by Carol Ballenger © 2020 Google

120

GUNNERSIDE

For Carol Ballenger

Place and way.
Stand for all.
A book
Always open
At its centre –
Half experience,
Half un-named hope.
Written on doing;
Mining
Farming
Building
Smithying
Clockmaking
Purveying.
Shown in
Stone
Gunnar's
Hill pasture,
Got of glacier,
Gill and Swale
Dale-dressed
In green and
Seasons;
Measured

WENSLEYDALE

Joseph Mallord William
Turner –
Romantic, the first
Modern Artist,
Illustrator
Of poets
And versemaker
Walked Wensleydale's
Broad and open
Miles
From end to end
Writing and sketching
For works
Of bliss-wrought
Genius
Homeless;
At home

To see clearly
Is poetry

Poet of light
And colour
And character
Prism-teased
The fallacies
Of hope
Alone

In the roiling
Roaring forces
Tumbling tales
Mill Gill
Water whelm; weather,
Fell and farm, barns
And the broad
Brush of Yore
That painted
In the detail
Of the Dale
Not set in
Blocked stone
But cleaved
To cascades;
Catch the
Necessary grace
Of their discourse
Out of time;
What nature
Imagines
A looking glass
Made of words
And the truest
History of the heart
Told

Holding true

J.M.W. TURNER AND WENSLEYDALE

From his notes, it seems that Turner often fuelled his walking and sketching trips with cheese, bread and beer.

Perhaps he took a satchel of supply from the Green Dragon Inn at Hardraw Scar – a welcoming hostelry that also hosted William Wordsworth who walked the dale too.

Did they ask why, singularly, Wensleydale isn't called Uredale, I wonder?

They might well have savoured earlier blue veined or sheep's milk Wensleydale cheese varieties from farmhouse dairies rather than today's classic white, mild but tangy mainstay.

That had to wait for Kit Calvert's twentieth century revival and the terrific Hawes based Wensleydale Creamery. I'm sure they'd have been in their element in the tasting shop!

'Mill Gill Fall, near Askrigg, Wensleydale' by J.M.W. Turner Turner Bequest, Tate Britain; digital photo © 2020 Tate

This page and opposite: 'Wensleydale Barns' by Martin Williamson © 2020 Martin Williamson

SUNSETS' SHADES – ROSEBERRY TOPPING

After Thomas Pierson and for Lynne

Even now
Remember.
Take five minutes
For the sunset
When it burns
Into being.
Is it special
For you?
Then soon it
Will be night
And cover for
Secrets
Shared with few
Or one
Only. Odin's
Broken hill
Made somehow
Complete
Your becoming
Profile
Distinct and
Distinctive
Shows your lineage
Of sandstones
Shot through
With iron
Now

From these vantage
Points
Below the
Summer house of
Childhood memory
Grown wild
With bluebell haze
And heather's bruise
Of beauty

Then the hour
Of pink, blue wash
Deepening
And burning gold
Setting left bronze
On hillflanks
Fleeting artefact;
Threshold time
Of softness
And some sadness
Longshadow;
Of the blurring
Of the edges
Of things.
It is the time
To watch this
Watercolour sky

Quietened
Until only
Last clouds
Still search
For shades of
Ochre and jet.

It could be me
It could be me

But not this night

Rise again

This page: 'Roseberry Topping with the Bluebells' by Lynne@SmoggieArt © *2020 SmoggieArt*
Opposite page: 'Roseberry Topping with the Shooting Lodge' by Lynne@SmoggieArt © *2020 SmoggieArt*

AFTERWORDS

I am, unavoidably, an unreliable narrator but it is in pursuit of a truth.
A memoir is like an innocent prisoner   best when freed

Conjugate 'To Belong'

Me, like?
As Grandad P
Would have put it -
'I belong Teesside';
Dear reader,
You/They belong
She/he belongs.
But not 'it'.
It's personal.

That doesn't mean
I'm there now
Or a lot of then
Maybe it means
I needed to leave
Anyway, but also
To give it
Some perspective
Timeloosened
Other landscapes
Wider horizons
To know how
It's defined -
Affinity;

A secure,
Close and intimate
Relationship.
A rage
A passion.
Mint

Not presence
Not distance
Not inverse
Snobbery
Not 'Little'
Not uncritical
But never cynical
And 'once'
Means 'always'
And always
With love.

I am of
That land
That sea
That language;
Word is....
I belong Teesside

John Powls
photograph by Graham Hodgson

'Relentless: Esk – Whitby' by William Tillyer © 2020 William Tillyer

ACKNOWLEDGEMENTS AND FURTHER INFORMATION

WILLIAM TILLYER – tillyer.com

'There is a quiet man who lives in the North. Many people think he is the finest painter in Britain. Many people may be right. His name is William Tillyer.'
Brian Appleyard CBE – *The Sunday Times*

Count me in as one of those 'many people'.

Middlesbrough born and North Yorkshire based, William Tillyer trained at Middlesbrough College of Art and The Slade and is an internationally renowned painter and printmaker with a career spanning sixty years.

His long time dealer, gallerist and friend, Bernard Jacobson believes William is coming into his best period now. Not bad when he is already widely regarded as one of the most significant painters in watercolour and, in my view, a pre-eminent artist of English landscape in any medium. His work is frequently exhibited nationally and internationally and is in the collections of major galleries worldwide.

William goes his own way and is rigorous and restless in moving on with his work, using the hardware of his art innovatively. One technique of pushing paint through an open grid, mesh 'canvas' from the back and shaping the image from what emerges resonates strongly with how I think about writing poetry.

His work is an ongoing dialogue between all aspects of nature and the nature of painting which continues an art historical timeline traced back through Matisse and Cezanne to Constable and Turner whose work he admires. A further dimension is set by the direction his work takes in the physical act of its creation.

As part of a series of events to celebrate his eightieth birthday he has recently collaborated on 'Nobody', illustrating a poem by Alice Oswald inspired by The Odyssey.

He has drawn career-long inspiration from the Esk Valley and the same land and seascapes that have inspired this collection of poems for me. I am very grateful to William for contributing his work to this book.

J. M. W. TURNER RA – tateimages.com

'The best of his peers ever admitted to his superiority in poetry, feeling, fancy and genius. They treated him with that reverential respect and estimation which is given to other artists by posterity alone. He is amongst the masters whose day is not so much of just today as of all time'.

That assessment from a measured obituary of Turner in The Times of December 1851 has stood the test of posterity – especially as regards his almost peerless work with landscapes and seascapes. He has claim to be the first modern artist, especially as regards his later watercolours which prefigure impressionism by decades.

I have long loved Turner's work and have often taken the thrilling opportunity to visit, view and research in the galleries and study rooms of the Turner Bequest collection at the Clore Gallery, Tate Britain.

His art is the key to a life of which many details yet remain elusive but we know he was a traveller and walker in pursuit of his art and visited North Yorkshire often. Not only was there poetry in his art but Turner illustrated the work of poets and also wrote poetry himself in the sketchbooks he always carried. The watercolours in this book are taken from those sketchbooks or follow up painted preparatory studies.

CAROL BALLENGER – artslive.org.uk

Photographer and musician, Carol Ballenger has been a collaborator of mine for more than twenty-five years. After first seeing her work in an exhibition, I contacted Carol and said, 'I'm writing poetry about what you're photographing' – and the rest is history! Her images are still inspiring me a quarter of a century on. Those herein were specially created for this book.

She works in landscape, both rural and urban, and produces archival quality, signed, limited edition photographs in her studio. She has exhibited widely and is a member of the Devon Guild of Craftsmen and a Fellow of the Royal Photographic Society.

She sees her work as meditations on the environment and often uses colour as an element of expression in its own right to emphasise the character of the image. Carol works with a digital camera and media but brings her darkroom skills to bear on the screen. She is the founder of Arts Live of which I am a member. I can think of no-one I'd rather work with on any arts project.

The images commissioned for this book develop a technique Carol used for our *Route 66* collaboration, using Google Earth and Streetview to replace her camera.

DAVID WATSON – thenorthernartist.co.uk

David Watson is a Teesside artist who, at time of writing, has recently achieved a long held ambition with a major show of his work at – suitably – the Dorman Museum in Middlesbrough. His work is in many public collections in the North East and nationally.

Like my Dad, he comes from the communities that were the backbone, hands and lungs of industrial Teesside. He knits together the loose industrial strands of the area with resonance and immediate recognition for those who have lived it and made it and those, like me, who have benefited from it or are drawn to know it.

I am grateful to David for his permission to use the images of his paintings that inspired me and to Mark Parham for organising to provide those.

RICHARD SPARE – richardspare.art

Artist and Master Printmaker, Richard Spare, is a long time collaborator of mine. He has, in the past, editioned work for many leading, contemporary artists such as David Hockney, Jasper Johns and Norman Ackroyd but now concentrates solely on his own very distinctive and evocative work which derives from nature and travel.

He is a frequent exhibitor at the Royal Academy Summer Exhibition and shows his work nationally and internationally with a particularly strong collector base in Japan where he visits often.

Much of Richard's work in this book has been specially created for the poems, 'Triptych For An Industrial Altar Piece – Renaissance', 'Harvest Perspectives' and 'Teenage Heartbreak' trilogy.

KAY SPARE – kayspare.com

Artist, writer and illustrator Kay Spare is a long time collaborator of mine and has responded to the 'IN SEA' poettes and the poem 'Harvest Perspectives' with watercolour sketches and paintings. The North Yorkshire coast was a much loved childhood holiday destination for Kay – and it shows in these images.

A brilliant colourist, her work here is typically vibrant and sensitive to the moods of the sea and landscape as well the emotions recalled that inspired me to write. In turn, her work has provoked me to write more. Kay's sense of design and experience in making her own books has also helped me place her work most effectively in the context of my book.

DAVID BELL – someseedifferent.com

David Bell is is a photographer, videographer and drone operator with strong Middlesbrough connections who utilises all the components of his creative process to achieve the best results for his clients. I first saw his stunning image of dawn over Teesside in the Middlesbrough Evening Gazette when working on this book and it inspired the poem 'Interpontes – Between The Bridges'.

David was working for a client, documenting a major civil engineering project when this opportunity arose. It's not just having the kit and the skills to use it – it's having 'the eye'. And David's certainly got that. 'It was an amazing sight as the sun came up over a place that is special to me', he said, 'and an opportunity to capture some landscape images from the view of the drone'.

IAN MITCHELL – ianmitchellart.com

Ian Mitchell is a North Yorkshire based artist who has exhibited extensively.

His 'linescapes' are a unique take on the landscapes he knows well with a stripped down approach to rendering what he sees. There are echoes of early 20th century travel posters and German and Swiss graphic design of the same period.

I first encountered his work on a visit to Whitby and immediately recognised the similarities to how I write poetry. I found his image of Sandsend Beach particularly evocative.

NORMAN ACKROYD CBE RA – normanackroyd.com

Norman Ackroyd CBE first emerged as a landscape artist with his works ranging from minimalist, near abstractions to detailed representational images in watercolour and etchings. He has exhibited extensively internationally and his work is in the collections of major galleries and museums worldwide. He was elected a member of the Royal Academy in 1988.

He has produced a stunning series of prints with subjects from his native Yorkshire landscape and seascape – amongst which is the image of Whitby Abbey in this book which I'm pleased to say is in my collection – and has also collaborated with poet, Kevin Crossley-Holland, contributing watercolours.

He was made CBE in 2007 for services to engraving and printing.

MACKENZIE THORPE – mackenziethorpe.net

If there was a public vote for such a thing as an 'official artist' of Teesside and North Yorkshire, I'm sure it would be Mackenzie Thorpe. In addition to his commercial work, Mackenzie frequently contributes to local charitable causes, organises local art initiatives and improves public spaces with his statues and displays of posters, for example.

One of the biggest selling British artists of the past thirty years, his distinctive work in several genres is rooted in the area with authenticity. Deeply emotive, it carries a message of hope that folks recognise and a style they appreciate.

His followers, collectors and exhibitors are national and international as well as local. He has been credited with changing the face of the UK art publishing market. He also enjoys writing poetry and his Arthaus Gallery is a lively presence in Richmond, North Yorkshire and on social media where it brightens many a day for lots of people.

EAMONN MCGOVERN – eamonnmcgovern.com

Eamonn McGovern M.A. (RCA) has been painting and sculpting all of his life and has worked as a professional artist for over thirty years. To date, he has shown his work in over fifty exhibitions in the U.K. and abroad.

He is part of the Platform Arts Project in Middlesbrough where his studio is based.

Every year, he designs a Christmas card to send to his daughter, Stephanie. This painting of the Acklam Hall Avenue Of Trees in the snow is the 2019 edition.

Steph proudly showed it off on her social media and I was inspired to a memory of my own and a poem.

Eamonn and Steph graciously consented to let me use the image alongside the poem for which I'm very grateful.

RJC MEDIA GROUP – DENNIS WELLER, CHRIS SCOTT WILSON AND GRAHAM LOWE
redcarjazzclubmedia.com

I am indebted to Dennis, Chris and Graham sparking some special memories and for some illustrative material from their book, 'Backstage Pass – Redcar Jazz Club' and to Dennis, especially, for all the help he gave me in getting that together.

'BEOWULF' – SEAMUS HEANEY AND DR JANINA RAMIREZ – janinaramirez.co.uk

My favourite modern interpretation of Beowulf is that by Nobel Laureate for Literature and poet, Seamus Heaney. It is a poetic work of art in its own right but, to me, gets closest to the spirit of the original both as a written piece and also when performed.

In recent years, Dr. Janina Ramirez has produced an accessible and authoritative book in the Ladybird Expert Series which gets to the essence of the Old English poem, it's language, world and context with the sort of passion and precision that my teacher, Miss Walker, epitomised all those years ago and which has stimulated me to pursue my interest even further.

LYNNE@SMOGGIEART – smoggieart.com

Lynne, the artist behind SmoggieArt, has one wish – for others to embrace both the natural beauty of and industrial landscape of Teesside and North Yorkshire just as she has in all her work rendered in black pen and pencils with her unique style which is quickly gaining her a following.

I discovered the image of 'The Masham' pub when researching for this book and it fitted so well with the poem of the same title – written 25 years ago.

I made contact with Lynne and she was kind enough to allow me to use that and several more of her splendid images which inspired yet more poems. The 'Window Of Opportunity' – Acklam Hall Library piece was specially commissioned for this project.

I share her wish. Grim up North? We think not.

THE EVENING GAZETTE – HELEN DALBY – gazettelive.co.uk

No appreciation of the 'landscape' of Teesside would be complete without images from the Evening Gazette archive, now managed as part of Mirrorpix. They've been telling the story of the town since 1869 in the print editions and, more recently, through TeessideLive on line.

My thanks for the use of the images in this book are due to Helen Dalby, Group Editor in Chief of *The Gazette* as part of Reach plc in the North East.

LINDSAY MULLEN – biniarrocagallery.com

I first saw Lindsay's beautiful post-impressionist paintings when I visited her lovely Biniarroca Studio and Gallery on Menorca over twenty years ago and bought some pieces from her. We began collaborating shortly after that.

An accomplished colourist, influenced by Turner and Monet, her palette and compositions reveal a refined sensitivity to the light and climate of the various locations in which she has lived and worked after graduating Fine Art in 1979 and moving to Menorca to continue her studies with an RA scholarship.

She now lives and works in Washington DC but continues to spend time in Menorca and her native UK. Her work is extensively exhibited and collected internationally.

Lindsay says, 'I focus on creating work that both captures my eye and enters my soul, so that a palpable inspiration has no choice but to emerge and be shared with others'. That's a sentiment I can strongly empathise with.

ANTHONY VICKERS – @untypicalboro

Self-described 'muliti-media, tub-thumping, tabloid rabble-rouser and citizen of the Peoples' Republic of Teesside', Vic – as he is known – was for thirty years 'Opinionated columnist and senior Boro (Middlesbrough FC) writer' for *Middlesbrough Evening Gazette*/TeessideLive until he left in August 2020 to pursue other opportunities.

He is acknowledged as one of the leading torch bearers for Teesside and describes his 'Untypicalboro' tumblr site as 'a pictorial love letter' to the place. That love is not blind, but love it is. He is a writer who has worked on the cusp where the most powerful and engaging forces of the 'Infant Hercules' meet. Who better, then, to pen a foreword for this collection – for which I am most grateful.

MARK SOFILAS – marksofilas.com

A native of Western Australia, Mark moved to Yorkshire in 2008 and changed his focus from being a commercial illustrator to taking up fine art with a body of work drawn from the North Yorkshire countryside and coast. His work is widely exhibited and collected.

His paintings are strongly guided by the emotions evoked for him by the scene and moment he is trying to capture and convey – the drift of smoke, a silhouette, shape or senses of history. It was those 'out of the ordinary' feelings that resonated with me as I was working on the poem his painting helped inspire.

JOHN P. POWLS

I became aware of my Dad's interest in art when, as a child at my Gran's house, I came across a book of his excellent drawings and paintings of World War II aircraft done from observation and back up by study during the war when he was in his early teens.

He later admitted that he would have liked to have gone to Art College but family finances demanded that he leave school at fourteen to begin his apprenticeship as an electrician and move into the world of work and, then, his National Service. He has said that he then became much more of a technical drawer than an artist and didn't actually take up brushes and paint again until middle age when he became an avid amateur landscape artist, working in watercolours and oils.

He kept this pursuit up until chronic, degenerative eye disease robbed him of sufficient sight to continue to work. Though he makes light of his sight loss, he often says that he misses doing his art most of all.

JUDITH A. POWLS

Ju is my splendid sister and sometime snap taker – a most capable lady, loved and looked to by family and her wide circle of friends.

For this project she has contributed much invaluable work as researcher, proof reader, 'critical friend', encourager and fount of knowledge about matters Teesside and environs as well as the photographs.

KEVIN FORTH – KevForthPhotography on Facebook

Kevin is a Teesside entrepreneur and keen photographer of his home area. I saw his striking image of the supermoon over Saltburn pier when it was being shared on social media across various Teesside and North Yorkshire groups. I contacted Kevin and was delighted that he consented for me to use it in this book. His Facebook page has many more fine examples of his work.

BENJAMIN ROBERT HAYDON/WILLIAM WORDSWORTH – npg.org.uk

Plymouth born, Haydon was a graduate of the Royal Academy Schools and a painter who specialised in grand historical pictures and some contemporary portraits – of which the portrait of Wordsworth reproduced in this book is one.

He had a somewhat tactless way with patrons which, coupled with his penchant for enormous scale in his works meant limited commercial success in his career. He was imprisoned for debt several times and, sadly, committed suicide in 1846, just four years after painting the Wordworth portrait.

PETER M. HICKS – petermhicks.co.uk

From his base in North Yorkshire, Peter has been a professional artist for many years and also headed up and lectured in large college art departments.

His perception and portrayal of local landscape moves between figuration and abstraction with the 'specifics' pared away in favour of mood, light, atmosphere and the rhythmic lie of the land. He sees himself as following in the line of the likes of Paul and John Nash, Sutherland and Piper in the way he deploys style, marks and colour in service of 'Romantic' landscape painting.

His beautiful 2020 collection is 'Entrance to a Lane' which was inspired by a Sutherland work of that name.

DR. PHIL BROWN – docbrown.info/docpics

'Doc' Phil Brown's travel pictures website is a positive cornucopia of images from all over the country and the world but especially of the area where he lives – North Yorkshire. He sees himself as a 'digital recorder-illustrator' and hopes that his images will encourage viewers to explore landscapes, seascapes and townscapes – either vicariously or, better still, in reality.

ANDREW GIFFORD – artuk.org/jmlondon.com

Born near Middlesbrough, Andrew is recognised as one of the most innovative landscape painters working today. His paintings and light installations are widely exhibited and collected nationally and internationally.

He has said that though he works internationally, he often feels the need to 're-charge his North-Easternness' by returning and painting there. He works 'on location' to produce his preliminary painted sketches that he later develops and finishes in his studio.

His strong townscapes – both abstract and figurative like those featured in this book – are often, rightly, described as beautiful and that he 'gets the place'. Andrew says that, if that is right, it is because he finds beauty in the places he paints.

TONY AND NICK WHELAN

Tony Whelan took the evocative photographs of Stockton Market in 1957 which show he had 'the eye' to compose an image.

They were provided to Stockton Picture Archive by his son, Nick. He has kindly permitted their use in my book and was good enough to provide the high quality versions needed.

PHILIP MEADOWS – philipmeadows.art

Born in the Teesside area, Philip studied at Cleveland Art College and Sunderland University focusing on sculpture and painting. He has completed many large commissions for both private and public organisations and has exhibited widely. Recently, his work has reflected the Teesside and North Yorkshire of his childhood and time spent on the moors and his mother's family farm.

I saw his evocative paintings of the Boro football grounds after seeing several as part of Middlesbrough FC's 'Art of Ayresome' online gallery, curated by Dr. Tosh Warwick to celebrate twenty-five years since the club moved out of the home ground it had occupied for over ninety years. Philip was kind enough to allow me to use images of two of his works in this book.

JACOB SHARPE – thehangingbadger.com & etsy.com/uk/shop/thehangingbadger

Jacob and I evidently share an interest in 'Beowulf'. The image in this book is taken from his illustrated account of the epic poem which I discovered in researching my book. It was made using vinyl-cut relief hand printing with water based black ink on high quality card.

More of his 'Beowulf' work and other prints, books and cards can be seen on his website and online shop.

L.S. LOWRY RA – thelowry.com

Although best known for industrial landscapes of his native North West, Lowry's work covers a wide range of themes and subjects from other landscapes and seascapes to portraits and surreal imaginings. His initial sketches were usually made outdoors, on the spot with the paintings done later in his workroom using his famously restricted palette of five colours.

His instantly recognisable work is now nationally and internationally famous and exhibited worldwide as well as in the Salford Gallery that bears his name.

In the late 1950's and 1960's he made repeated visits to the North East where he drew and, later, painted many seascapes as well as the work featured in this book which was acquired by the Friends of Middlesbrough Art Gallery and is now in the permanent collection of the Middlesbrough Institute of Modern Art.

MARTIN WILLIAMSON – cobbybrook.co.uk & @cobbybrook

Martin is a Yorkshire artist whose work is in a number of private collections worldwide and those of several institutions in the UK. It has been featured in numerous publications and online outlets as well as in his own lively social media presence. He has published a collaborative book – 'Recollections' – with poet Giles Watson which is available to buy online via his website.

He says, 'To me, my works are a natural conclusion to an interaction with the landscape. They are the result of time spent in the elements – walking, sketching, painting, remembering.' Recently, his images of churches have been described by Prof. Alice Roberts as, 'Piper-esque'.

I saw Martin's images of Wensleydale barns on his Twitter feed and he was gracious enough to contribute them to the book.

MATT WHITFIELD – mattwhitfieldart.co.uk

Matt was born on Teesside and has returned to live there after his successful 22 year Army career to pursue his artistic goals.

He chose to paint his home area not out of nostalgia for some bygone era but to celebrate all the varied aspects of its beauty today and its people. He is also inspired by other local artists.

To capture the raw, stark beauty of his distinctive and evocative landscapes, Matt works primarily in charcoal and soft pastels with a limited palette.

THANKS ARE ALSO DUE TO

Stockton-On-Tees Council Picture Archive; The British Library; British Steel and successors; Francis Frith Collection; Tate Britain Studyroom; Clore Gallery, Tate Britain; National Portrait Gallery; Middlesbrough Institute Of Modern Art; and, Wensleydale Creamery - wensleydale.co.uk. Specially, my longtime publishers - Halsgrove and their Associate Publisher and my editor/publisher of twenty-five years standing, Simon Butler

BOOKS

Backstage Pass – Redcar Jazz Club. Dennis Weller, Chris Scott Wilson & Graham Lowe, 2015 RJC Media Group.

Beowulf. Janina Ramirez, 2020 A Ladybird Expert Book.

Beowulf. Seamus Heaney, 1999 Faber & Faber.

Nobody. Alice Oswald and William Tillyer, 2018 21 Publishing.

William Tillyer – Loneliness of the Long Distance Runner. Bernard Jacobson, 2018 21 Publishing.

Entrance to a Lane. Peter M. Hicks, 2020 Peter M. Hicks.

Song Of The Earth. Jonathan Bate, 2001 Picador.

Radical Wordsworth: The Poet Who Changed The World. Jonathan Bate, 2020 William Collins.

The Living Mountain. Nan Shepherd, 1977 Aberdeen University Press.

Landmarks. Robert Macfarlane, 2015 Hamish Hamilton.

The Making Of Poetry: Coleridge, The Wordsworths And Their Year Of Marvels. Adam Nicholson, 2019 William Collins.

Leaves of Grass. Walt Whitman, 1867 edition reprinted by Amazon e-books.

Sea To The West. Norman Nicholson, 1981 Faber & Faber.

Constable's Skies. Dr. Mark Evans, 2018 Victoria and Albert Museum/Thames and Hudson.

The Place Names of Yorkshire. Paul Chrystal, 2017 Stenlake Publishing Limited.

Secret Middlesbrough. Paul Chrystal & Stan Laundon, 2015 Amberley Publishing.

Middlesbrough 1920–2020 A Century Of Change. Araf Chohan, 2019 DestinWorld Publishing.

A Cheesemonger's History Of The British Isles. Ned Palmer, 2019 Profile Books.

'The Old Town Hall and St. Hilda's Church' by L.S. Lowry

142

ST. HILDA'S

For L.S. Lowry, Bolckow & Vaughan

Rarely
Went
Over
The
Border

―――

Wrong
Side
Of
The
Tracks?

―――

But
From
What
Stand
Point?

―――

Origin
Story;
Chance
Of
Renaissance

Small
Figures
With
Big
Ideas
In
A
Townscape
Growing

'The real journey of discovery consists not only in seeking new landscapes
but in seeing our landscapes anew'

Marcel Proust